Practice and problems
in advanced mathematics

D1471666

The School Mathematics Project

CAMBRIDGE
UNIVERSITY PRESS

Author   Colin Goldsmith

Project Director   Stan Dolan

The author would like to thank Laurence Ellis for his constructive criticism and checking of solutions and Ann White for her help in preparing this book for publication.

Published by the Press Syndicate of the University of Cambridge
The Pitt Building, Trumpington Street, Cambridge CB2 1RP
40 West 20th Street, New York, NY 10011–4211, USA
10 Stamford Road, Oakleigh, Melbourne 3166, Australia

© Cambridge University Press 1994

First published 1994
Reprinted 1995

Produced by 16–19 Mathematics, Southampton

Printed in Great Britain by Scotprint Ltd, Musselburgh

ISBN 0 521 45561 8 paperback

Notice to teachers

Contents

Introduction

The material in the exercises of this book has been chosen carefully to enhance skills of manipulation in algebra and calculus within stimulating contexts closely related to those in A level mathematics courses. The book can be used wholly or in part by one or more students working independently, and so provide a variable amount of enrichment for those who may work more rapidly than their classmates or who may wish to put in extra time and effort. The answers given are intended to be full enough so that teacher input need not be excessive.

The *16–19 Mathematics* course harnesses the potential of graphical, programmable calculators to reduce the amount of complicated algebra required and highlight the power and range of the underlying concepts. The course thus aims to be attractive and accessible to a broader spectrum of ability. This new book should be suitable for all high attaining students but should be especially valuable for students on the *16–19 Mathematics* course aiming for entry to Oxford and Cambridge Universities.

The following notes on individual sections may be of use. Relevant *16–19 Mathematics* texts are cross-referenced in brackets.

Sigma notation and series (*Foundations*)

This section provides considerable practice in basic algebra and concentrates in particular on the method of differences.

Maximum and minimum points (*Introductory calculus*)

Work with a graph plotter is linked with alternative methods using algebra and calculus. Differentiation of polynomial functions is extended to fractional powers of x.

Parabolic and elliptical reflectors (*Introductory calculus*)

A guided project develops important properties of the parabola and ellipse. Numerical work leads gently to more complicated algebraic generalisations.

Solving equations (*Functions*)

Ideas of inverse functions, graphs, solution of equations and iterative methods are applied to a variety of functions. Students are encouraged to use simple programs.

Adding vectors (*Newton's laws of motion*)

Simple vector work is extended through the use of polar-rectangular conversion.

Vector triangles (*Newton's laws of motion*)

Forces and velocities provide the main applications for this section which emphasises trigonometric calculations based upon vector diagrams.

Mean and variance formulas (*Living with uncertainty*)

This short section provides algebraic proofs of alternative formulas for variance.

Sampling without replacement (*Living with uncertainty*)

The most important sampling ideas are reinforced in various contexts. A computer or graphical calculator could be used to produce effective simulations.

Sine and cosine rules (*Mathematical methods*)

This section provides consolidation of these two rules together with a detailed scrutiny of the ambiguous case of the sine rule.

Trigonometric identities (*Mathematical methods*)

Familiarity with the addition formulas and double angle formulas is gained through their study in the context of geometry, algebra and calculus.

Further trigonometry (*Mathematical methods*)

The identities of the previous section are used in an extended practical context together with some useful practice in numerical analysis.

Air resistance (*Mathematical methods*)

The basic ideas of differential equations are linked together in their application to a simple model of motion in one dimension with air resistance proportional to speed.

Tan and sec (*Calculus methods*)

This section brings together many calculus ideas connected with the tangent and secant functions.

Calculus techniques (*Calculus methods*)

This section gives valuable practice in the skill of choosing an appropriate integration technique.

Polynomial approximations (*Calculus methods*)

Standard polynomial approximations are applied, especially in the integration of awkward functions. Some programming is encouraged in later questions.

Sigma notation and series

The two most important sequences are arithmetic and geometric progressions but there is a wide variety of other sequences and series. This exercise develops ways of extending the repertoire and provides some important formulas.

1   Write out in full and simplify $\displaystyle\sum_{1}^{4} (\sqrt{(i+1)} - \sqrt{i})$.

Repeat for $\displaystyle\sum_{1}^{5} \left[(i+1)^2 - i^2 \right]$.

Explain why $\displaystyle\sum_{1}^{n} \left[f(i+1) - f(i) \right] = f(n+1) - f(1)$ for any function f.

2   Take $f(x) = x^2$ in the final result of question 1 and show that $\displaystyle\sum_{1}^{n} (2i+1) = (n+1)^2 - 1$. Check this for $n = 3$.

3   Take $f(x) = (x-1)^2$ instead and show that $\displaystyle\sum_{1}^{n} (2i-1) = n^2$. How is this result related to the diagram below?

X	O	X	O	X
X	O	X	O	O
X	O	X	X	X
X	O	O	O	O
X	X	X	X	X

4   By taking $f(x) = (x-1)x$, show that $\displaystyle\sum_{1}^{n} i = \frac{1}{2} n(n+1)$.

5   If $f(x) = (x-1)x(x+1)$, show that $f(i+1) - f(i) = 3i(i+1)$ and hence that

$$\sum_{1}^{n} i(i+1) = \frac{1}{3} n(n+1)(n+2).$$

6   Show by the methods of questions 4 and 5 that

$$\sum_{1}^{n} i(i+1)(i+2) = \frac{1}{4} n(n+1)(n+2)(n+3).$$

7   Complete the working: $\displaystyle\sum_{1}^{n} i^2 = \sum_{1}^{n} [i(i+1) - i]$

$$= \frac{1}{3} n(n+1)(n+2) - \frac{1}{2} n(n+1)$$

$$= \frac{1}{6} n(n+1) [\ \ldots\ -\ \ldots\ ]$$

$$= \frac{1}{6} n(n+1)(2n+1)$$

8 Write down the first four terms of the series $\sum_1^n (i-1)\, i\, (i+1)$ and (using question 6) show that its sum is $\frac{1}{4}\,(n-1)\, n\, (n+1)(n+2)$.

Then find a formula for $\sum_1^n i^3$ by expressing it as $\sum_1^n \left[(i-1)\, i\, (i+1) + i \right]$

Show that your answer simplifies to $\frac{1}{4}\, n^2\, (n+1)^2$.

9 Taking $f(x) = x^3$, show that $\sum_1^n (3i^2 + 3i + 1) = (n+1)^3 - 1$ and hence that

$$\sum_1^n i^2 = \frac{1}{3}\left[n^3 + 3n^2 + 3n - 3\sum_1^n i - n \right]$$

Use this to obtain the result of question 7 by another method.

10 Show that $i^4 = (i-1)\, i\, (i+1)(i+2) - 2i^3 + i^2 + 2i$

$$= (i-1)\, i\, (i+1)(i+2) - 2(i-1)\, i\, (i+1) + i^2.$$

Deduce an expression for $\sum_1^n i^4$. Do not simplify it but check your answer by taking n equal to 2 or 3.

11 (a) Use the formula for $\sum_1^n i^2$ to show that $n(n+1)(2n+1)$ is divisible by 6.

   (b) How could you demonstrate this result in a different way?

12 Obtain formulas for: (a) $\sum_{n+1}^{2n} i^2$, (b) $\sum_n^{2n} i^3$, giving your answers in factorised form.

Use a simple check.

13 Sum the series:

   (a) $1^2 + 3^2 + 5^2 + \ldots + (2n-1)^2$

   (b) $2^2 + 4^2 + 6^2 + \ldots + (2n)^2$

Show that the sum of your answers to (a) and (b) simplifies to give the formula for $\sum_1^{2n} i^2$.

14 Given $S_n = \sum_1^n \frac{1}{i(i+1)}$, work out S_1, S_2, S_3 and S_4 as simple fractions and suggest a formula for S_n. Can you prove it correct?

Maximum and minimum points

Although it is possible to get all the information you need about a specific function from a graphical calculator, it is worthwhile to sketch graphs and find maximum and minimum points using only algebra and calculus.

1. For each of the following, use a graph plotter to find approximately the coordinates of the maximum and minimum points.

   (a) $y = (4 + x)(7 - x)$

   (b) $y = x^2 (x - 5)$

   (c) $y = x (x - 5)^2$

   (d) $y = (x + 1)(x - 4)^2$

   (e) $y = (x + 4)(x - 1)(x - 3)$

   (f) $y = (x + 1)(x - 1)(x - 6)$

2. For each of the following, write down where the graphs meet the coordinate axes, sketch the graphs without using a graph plotter and find the maximum and minimum points.

   (a) $y = (2x + 3)(x - 5)$

   (b) $y = (3x - 7)^2$

   (c) $y = x (2x - 9)^2$

   (d) $y = (x + 2)(x - 3)(x - 5)$

   (e) $y = x (2x + 1)(2x - 3)$

3. Use a graph plotter to show that $x^3 - 2x + 6 = 0$ has only one real root while $x^3 - 6x + 2 = 0$ has three roots.

   Find how many real roots each of the following cubic equations has.

   (a) $x^3 - 3x + 1 = 0$

   (b) $x^3 - 3x + 2 = 0$

   (c) $x^3 - 3x + 3 = 0$

4. Without using a graph plotter, find the maximum and minimum points (if any) of the following.

   (a) $y = x^3 - 12x + 7$

   (b) $y = x^3 - 12x - 17$

   (c) $y = x^3 + 12x + 17$

   How many real roots are there for the following equations?

   (d) $x^3 - 12x + 7 = 0$

   (e) $x^3 - 12x - 17 = 0$

   (f) $x^3 + 12x + 17 = 0$

5. Show that $x^3 - ax + b = 0$ has three real roots only if $b^2 < \dfrac{4a^3}{27}$.

6   Explain why the graph of $y = \sqrt{x}$ is a reflection of half of the graph of $y = x^2$.

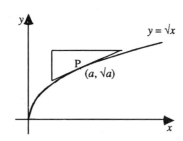

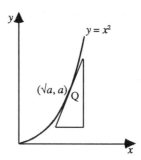

Find the gradient at Q for the second graph. Deduce the gradient at P for the first graph.

It should follow that if $y = \sqrt{x}$, then $\frac{dy}{dx} = \frac{1}{2\sqrt{x}}$.

7   Repeat question 1 for:

    (a) $y = x - \sqrt{x}$ (b) $y = x - 10\sqrt{x}$

    (c) $y = x + \sqrt{x}$ (d) $y = x^2 - 8\sqrt{x}$

Then obtain accurate answers by differentiation and algebra.

8   Use the method of question 6 to differentiate $\sqrt[3]{x}$.

9   Find cubic functions with graphs as shown below.

    (a)

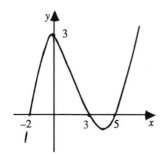

    (b)

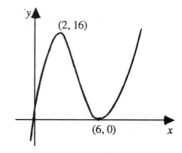

    (c)

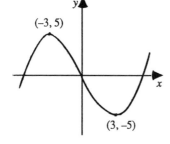

    (d)

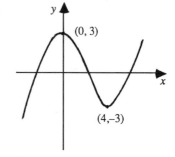

4

(e)

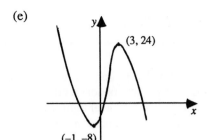

10 This is the graph of a cubic function with the origin as a minimum point. Show that the ratio of the areas A_1 and A_2 is 16 : 11.

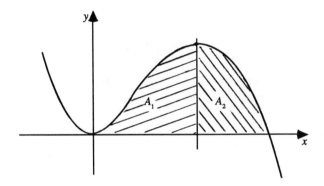

Parabolic and elliptical reflectors

It is well-known that radio telescopes, satellite dishes and car headlamps contain reflectors with a parabolic shape. This exercise develops the reason for this. As a mathematical model, consider an idealised light source concentrated at the point F in the diagram. A typical light ray is shown and the laws of physics say that at the point of reflection P, the angles α and β made with the tangent are equal.

For each parabola, there is a single point F with the property that the light rays are reflected parallel to the axis of the parabola; it is called the focus. In question 3, you will see how to find the focus.

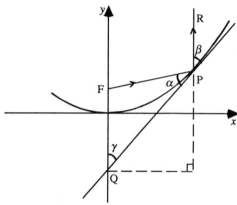

1   Let the parabola have equation $y = \frac{1}{4}x^2$, and F be (0, 1). Suppose P has x-coordinate 6.
     Find the y-coordinate of P, the gradient of the graph at P and the lengths FP and FQ.
     Deduce that the reflected ray PR is parallel to the y-axis.

2   Repeat question 1 if the x-coordinate of P is:

     (a)   10   (b)   4   (c)   2

     If P is the point $(t, \frac{1}{4}t^2)$, show that FP $= \frac{1}{4}t^2 + 1$ and complete the working to show that
     the reflected ray is parallel to the y-axis.

3

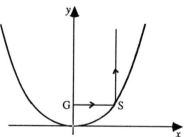

     This shows a different parabola. If a ray from G parallel to the x-axis is reflected parallel
     to the y-axis, what is the gradient of the parabola at S?

     What are the coordinates of G if the equation of the curve is:

     (a) $y = x^2$ (b) $y = 3x^2$?

     In each case prove the light property by the method of question 2.

4   Repeat question 3 for the parabola $y = kx^2$.

5   The graph of $16x^2 + 25y^2 = 400$ is the ellipse shown in (a). It is the result of a one-way stretch applied to the circle through A, C and U.

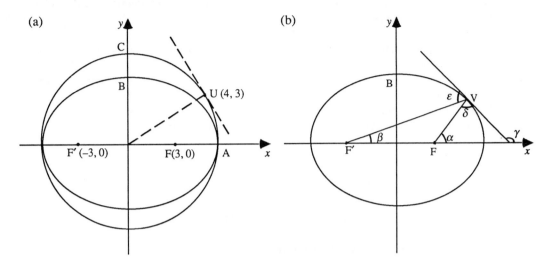

(a)   (b)

Find the coordinates of A and B, and hence the scale factor of the stretch. If U is the point (4, 3) on the circle, show (without using calculus) that the gradient at U is $-\frac{4}{3}$. Find the coordinates of V (the image of U under the stretch) and the gradient of the ellipse at V. If F is (3, 0) and F′ is (− 3, 0), find, to 1 decimal place, the angles marked α, β, γ, δ and ε on (b). Explain why a ray of light from F would be reflected by the ellipse through F′.

Calculate also the lengths FV and F′V.

6   Repeat question 5 for different positions of U. Display your results in a copy of this table.

x-coordinate of U	U	V	Gradient at V	δ	ε	FV	F′V
1							
2							
3							
4	(4, 3)	(4, 2.4)	$-\frac{4}{3}$ x 0.8	65.8°	65.8°	2.6	7.4

Comment on your answers.

7   In question 6, if the x-coordinate of U is t, show that FV $= \dfrac{25 - 3t}{5}$ and F′V $= \dfrac{25 + 3t}{5}$.

If instead the ellipse has equation $b^2x^2 + a^2y^2 = a^2b^2$, F is $(c, 0)$, F′ is $(-c, 0)$, $c = \sqrt{(a^2 - b^2)}$ and V has x-coordinate equal to t, show that FV $= a - \dfrac{ct}{a}$ and find the length of F′V.

8   Explain the method of drawing an ellipse using drawing pins and a loop of string.

Solving equations

The key ideas of inverse functions, graphs, solution of equations and iterative methods are applied to a variety of functions.

1 Use the appropriate inverse functions to solve these equations to 3 significant figures.

    (a) $x^5 = 32$ (b) $x^5 = 28.1$ (c) $\log x = 2.15$
    (d) $10^x = 35.9$ (e) $\ln x = 3.33$ (f) $e^x = 1.68$
    (g) $\sin^{-1}x = 3.92$ (radian mode)
    (h) $\sin x = 0.444$ (Give all the answers between 0 and 10.)

2 Use inverse functions to solve to 3 significant figures:

    (a) $7 \sqrt{(\tfrac{1}{2}x + 3)} = 19.7$ (b) $4 \log (2x + 1) = 0.656$
    (c) $3 \ln (4x - 5) = 6.78$ (d) $5 e^{4x} = 3.21$
    (e) $9 \cos (5t) = 6.02$ (Give all the answers between -2 and 2.)

3 Make x the subject of the following formulas:

    (a) $y = 7\sqrt{(\tfrac{1}{2}x + 3)}$ (b) $y = 4 \log (2x + 1)$
    (c) $y = 5 e^{4x}$ (d) $y = 2 \ln 8x + 6$

4 Sketch on the same axes the graphs of $y = x$ and $y = 2^{-x}$. Use the program to solve iteratively, to 3 significant figures, the equation $x = 2^{-x}$ starting with $x = 0$. Illustrate how the process works either on your sketch or with graphs drawn on your calculator screen

CASIO	TEXAS
$? \rightarrow X$	Input X
Lbl 1	Lbl 1
$2x^y (-X) \rightarrow X \blacktriangle$	$2 \wedge (-X) \rightarrow X$
Goto 1	Disp X
	Goto 1

5 Repeat question 4 for the following equations, choosing suitable starting values.

    (a) $x = 3 \ln x$ (b) $x = 3^{-x} + 1$
    (c) $x = \sin x + 1$ (d) $x = x + 3^{-x} - 0.5$

6 Show that question 5(d) solves the equation $3^x = 2$. Obtain this solution more directly using logarithms.

Program the iteration $x_{i+1} = x_i + 3^{x_i} - 2$ with $x_1 = 1$. Why does this not converge on the solution of $3^x = 2$?

7 The graphs of $y = x$ and $y = 3 \ln x$ meet at two points (see question 5(a)). Which solution of $x = 3 \ln x$ is given by the obvious iteration?

Show that the equation is equivalent to $x = e^{x/3}$ and that the iteration $x_{i+1} = e^{x_i/3}$ gives the other solution. Show simultaneously on your calculator screen the graphs of $y = x$, $y = 3 \ln x$ and $y = e^{x/3}$.

8 Find both solutions of the equation $x = e^x - 2$ using two different iterations. Illustrate with sketch graphs.

9 Show that the equation $x^3 - 3x + 1 = 0$ has three real roots and locate them roughly from a graph.

Write the equation in the form $x = f(x)$, where $f(x) = \dfrac{x^3 + 1}{3}$ and then find $f^{-1}(x)$.

Show simultaneously on your calculator screen the graphs of $y = x$, $y = f(x)$ and $y = f^{-1}(x)$.

From the iterations $x_{i+1} = f(x_i)$ and $x_{i+1} = f^{-1}(x_i)$ and with suitable starting values, obtain to 5 significant figures all three solutions of the original equation. What do you notice about the answers?

10 An extended problem

Most of the techniques required for this investigation are elementary, so little guidance is given. You will have to show some initiative.

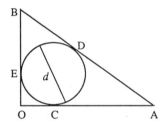 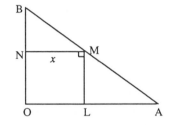 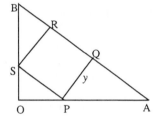

The diagrams all show a right-angled triangle OAB. In the first, a circle of diameter d cm is inscribed. The others contain squares of sides x and y cm.

(a) If the triangle has sides 3, 4, 5 cm, find d, x, y and compare the areas of the circle and the two squares.

(b) If the triangle has fixed hypotenuse h cm and variable angle OAB = θ radians, find d as a function of θ and sketch the graph. Show the maximum value of d, and find the gradient at the origin.

(c) Use the triangle of part (b) to find x as a function of θ. Sketch the graph and show the maximum point. By considering $\dfrac{x}{\theta}$ for small θ, find the gradient at the origin.

(d) Repeat part (c) for y.

(e) Show that $x > y$ for all θ between 0 and $\dfrac{\pi}{2}$.

(f) Show that $d > x$ for all θ between 0 and $\dfrac{\pi}{2}$.

(g) Is the area of the circle always greater than the area of the square of side x?

Adding vectors

A vector can be expressed in **rectangular** (Cartesian) form, as in the first diagram, or in **polar** form, as in the second diagram.

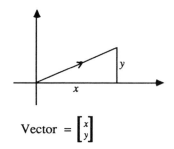

Vector = $\begin{bmatrix} x \\ y \end{bmatrix}$

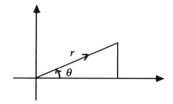

Vector has length r at an angle θ anticlockwise from the x-axis

It is easy to calculate the rectangular components from the polar ones.

$$x = r \cos \theta, \ y = r \sin \theta$$

Reversing the process,

$$r = \sqrt{(x^2 + y^2)}, \ \tan \theta = \frac{y}{x},$$

but the angle θ must be considered carefully from a diagram if either x or y (or both) is negative.

It is easier to use a calculator. Check that it has buttons for conversion from rectangular to polar form and vice versa; if you are not already familiar with them, find out how to use them.

1   Convert the vector $\begin{bmatrix} 5 \\ 3 \end{bmatrix}$ to polar form using the equations above.

Check that the calculator function gives the same answers.

Use the calculator function to convert the following vectors to polar form. Check that the answers are reasonable.

(a) $\begin{bmatrix} 3 \\ 5 \end{bmatrix}$ (b) $\begin{bmatrix} 0 \\ 10 \end{bmatrix}$ (c) $\begin{bmatrix} -11 \\ 6 \end{bmatrix}$ (d) $\begin{bmatrix} 11 \\ -6 \end{bmatrix}$ (e) $\begin{bmatrix} -3 \\ -4 \end{bmatrix}$

2   Using the equations above, check that a vector of length 5 at 60° to the x-axis equals $\begin{bmatrix} 2.5 \\ 4.33 \end{bmatrix}$. Obtain the same answers from the calculator function.

Convert the following vectors to rectangular form. Check that the positive and negative signs are as you would expect.

(a)   Length 2.8 at 36°   (b)   Length 7.3 at 180°

(c)   Length 18 at 152°   (d)   Length 18 at –28°

(e)   Length 18 at 332°   (f)   Length 25 at 225°

(g)   Length 5.1 at 270°   (h)   Length 123 at –104°

3

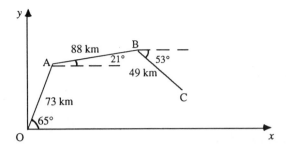

A helicopter flies from O to A, and then on to B and C, as shown in the diagram. Express each stage of the journey in rectangular form, add the three vectors and find the distance OC and the angle that OC makes with the x-axis. Check all your answers using a scale drawing.

4   Three forces act on a body as illustrated in the diagram. Together they are equivalent to a single force which can be found as in question 3. Find the magnitude and direction of this 'resultant force'. Draw a diagram like that in question 3 as a check.

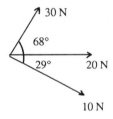

5   Repeat question 4 for the following systems.

(a)   (b)

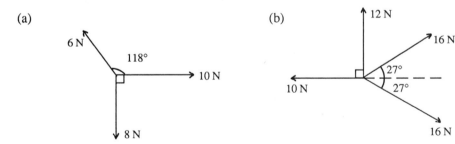

You will have noticed that the mathematician's definition of polar coordinates differs from the range and bearing commonly used in geography and navigation. You can convert bearings to angles anticlockwise from the x-axis and vice versa. Alternatively, if the calculator functions are used directly, the first rectangular component is the North component and the second is the East component. You are recommended to use diagrams to check that your answers are plausible.

6   Express the following velocities as column vectors:

(a)   350 km h⁻¹ on a course of 104°

(b)   350 km h⁻¹ on a course of 076°

(c)   400 km h⁻¹ on a course of 292°

(d)   500 km h⁻¹ on a course of 213°

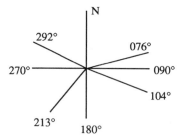

7   A plane flies with airspeed 550 km h⁻¹ on a compass course of 069°. There is a wind of speed 60 km h⁻¹ **from** a direction of 192°. Express both of these as column vectors, add them and by converting to polar form find the 'speed made good' and the actual course followed by the plane.

8   Repeat question 7 for the following:

(a)   Airspeed = 400 km h⁻¹, course set = 143°, wind 80 km h⁻¹ from 180°

(b)   Airspeed = 600 km h⁻¹, course set = 308°, wind 50 km h⁻¹ from 154°

(c)   Airspeed = 800 km h⁻¹, course set = 227°, wind 70 km h⁻¹ from 083°

Vector triangles

Two or more vectors (representing displacement, velocity, acceleration, force or momentum) may be combined in rectangular form or by drawing or by calculation from a sketch diagram. This exercise concentrates on calculation from sketch diagrams. If you know the sine and cosine rules for a triangle, they may be used if you prefer.

1 The diagram shows a displacement of 90 km followed by another of 65 km in the directions shown.

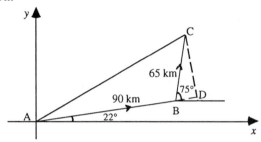

Calculate the angle CBD, then the lengths CD, BD, AD and AC. Finally find the angle CAD.

Check your last two answers by expressing **AB**, **BC**, **AC** as column vectors and then finding **AC** in polar form.

2 Use the second diagram to calculate the size and direction of the resultant of the two forces shown.

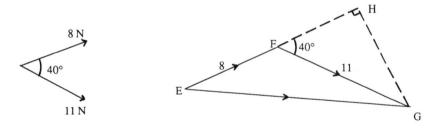

3 Repeat question 2 for the following pairs of forces, drawing your own vector triangles.

(a)   (b)

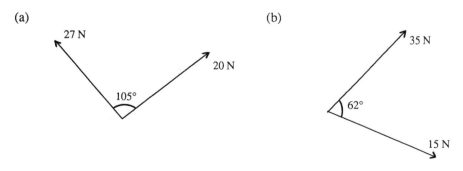

4   The diagram shows how a plane's airspeed of 400 km h^{-1}, on a course of 048°, combines with a wind of 70 km h^{-1} from a direction 090°.

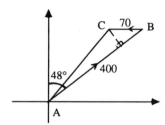

Use the diagram to calculate the speed and course made good, i.e. the length and direction of **AC**.

5   Suppose you wish to travel in the direction of 010° and the wind and airspeed are as in question 4. Then the relevant diagram is as drawn. Calculate the course to steer (the direction of **AB**) and the speed made good (the length of **AC**).

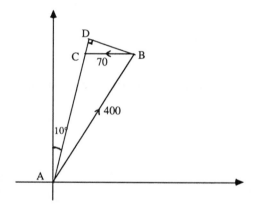

6   Repeat question 5 for the following data, first drawing relevant vector triangles.

(a)   Airspeed = 500 km h^{-1}; combined course to be due East; wind 60 km h^{-1} from 333°

(b)   Airspeed = 500 km h^{-1}; combined course to be 070°; wind as in (a)

(c)   Airspeed = 300 km h^{-1}; combined course to be 190°; wind 50 km h^{-1} from due west

(d)   Airspeed = 400 km h^{-1}; combined course to be 152°; wind 60 km h^{-1} from 055°

Mean and variance formulas

The variance of n numbers can be expressed both as $\dfrac{\sum (x - \bar{x})^2}{n}$ and as $\dfrac{\sum x^2}{n} - \bar{x}^2$. A proof that these expressions are equivalent is developed in question 1.

1   Writing m in place of $\bar{x}$, complete the following:

$$\frac{1}{n} \sum (x - m)^2 = \frac{1}{n} \sum (x^2 \dots)$$

$$= \frac{1}{n} [\sum x^2 - \sum \dots + \sum \dots]$$

$$= \frac{1}{n} [\sum x^2 - 2m \sum \dots + \dots]$$

$$= \frac{1}{n} [\sum x^2 - 2m \times \dots + \dots]$$

$$= \frac{1}{n} [\sum x^2 - m^2 n \ ]$$

$$= \frac{1}{n} \sum x^2 - m^2$$

2   With a frequency distribution, the variance is defined as:

$$\frac{1}{n} \sum (x - m)^2 f \text{ where } n = \sum f \text{ and } m = \frac{1}{n} \sum xf.$$

Prove algebraically, as in question 1, that the variance can be written as $\dfrac{1}{n} \sum x^2 f - m^2$.

3   For a probability model, the variance is defined by:

$$\sum (x - \mu)^2 \, P(x) \text{ where } \sum P(x) = 1 \text{ and } \mu = \sum x \, P(x).$$

Write out the algebraic proof that the variance can be written as $\sum x^2 \, P(x) - \mu^2$.

4   Show algebraically that reducing each number in a frequency distribution by a fixed amount k does not alter the variance.

5   A set of 10 numbers has mean 14 and standard deviation 6. Find the sum of the squares of the numbers.

A second set contains 15 numbers with mean 19 and standard deviation 4.

Find the mean and standard deviation of all 25 numbers combined to make a single population.

Sampling without replacement

For this exercise you will need some marbles or counters or pegs, identical except for colour. The experiments are ideal for groupwork, large samples being formed by several individuals pooling results. Alternatively, a computer could be used to produce an effective simulation.

1 10 marbles are placed in a bag. 4 are red and the rest are blue. 3 marbles are removed and the number of reds is recorded. These are replaced in the bag which is then shaken and the procedure is repeated 50 times. The results are as follows:

Number of reds	Number of samples
0	7
1	22
2	17
3	4
	50

Carry out a similar experiment. Find the mean and standard deviation of the number of reds from both the sample above and your own.

Complete the tree diagram below and hence find the predicted frequencies from 50 trials based on the probability model.

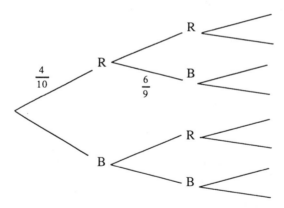

Find the mean and variance from the probability model.

2 Repeat question 1 starting with 3 red and 7 blue marbles (or equivalent equipment).

3   Start with 2 red and 8 blue marbles. Select one marble at a time without replacement until a red marble is chosen. Record the number of marbles required to obtain a red (e.g. for the sequence BBBR record the number 4; for BR record 2). What is the smallest number you might record? What is the largest? What do you anticipate will be the mean score?

Carry out 90 trials, returning the marbles to the bag and shaking well between trials. Display your results in a frequency table and find the mean.

From a tree diagram, or otherwise, find the probabilities of each score, the predicted frequencies from a total of 90 trials and the predicted mean. Compare with the observed values.

4   Repeat question 3, replacing each marble in the bag after noting its colour.

5   Suggest what results you would expect if question 3 is repeated starting with:

(a)   4 red and 16 blue marbles,

(b)   20 red and 80 blue marbles.

6   Repeat question 1 'with replacement', i.e. for each trial take 1 marble, note its colour, return it to the bag, shake the bag and repeat three times.

7   Are political opinion poll samples chosen with or without replacement? Does it matter?

8   A die is thrown repeatedly until an even number is obtained. What is the probability that this takes 4 throws? How many throws will be needed on average?

Answer the same questions if the die is thrown until a six appears.

9   Find out about the St. Petersburg paradox.

Sine and cosine rules

The sides and angles of a triangle which is not right-angled are connected by the formulas known as the sine and cosine rules.

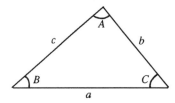

$$\frac{a}{\sin A} = \frac{b}{\sin B} = \frac{c}{\sin C}$$

$a^2 = b^2 + c^2 - 2bc \cos a$, which may also be written in the form

$$\cos A = \frac{b^2 + c^2 - a^2}{2bc}$$

In this section you will be using these formulas to answer a variety of questions.

1   Estimate the length a when:

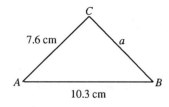

   (a)   angle $A = 12.5°$

   (b)   angle $A = 83.3°$

   (c)   angle $A = 156.1°$

   Calculate the lengths to 3 s.f. using the cosine rule.

2   For the triangle in question 1, find angle A to 1 d.p. when:

   (a) $a = 6.4$ cm   (b) $a = 15.7$ cm

3

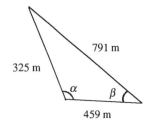

   (a)   What does the cosine rule give for:

      (i) $\cos \alpha$ (ii) α?

      Explain your answer to (ii).

   (b)   What does the cosine rule give for $\cos \beta$?

4 Use the sine rule to find x when:

(a) $\alpha = 48°$

(b) $\alpha = 74°$

(c) $\alpha = 106°$

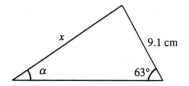

Comment on your answers.

5 For the triangle of question 4, find α when:

(a) $x = 11.8$ cm

(b) $x = 8.4$ cm (there are two answers)

(c) $x = 7.7$ cm

6 Draw two triangles with different shapes, each with $a = 5.5$ cm, $b = 6.8$ cm, $A = 49°$. Find the other side and angles:

(a) using the sine rule;

(b) using the cosine rule and solving the resulting quadratic equation.

7 Two spheres have radii 10 cm and 8 cm and their centres are 13 cm apart. Find the radius of the circle in which they intersect.

8 An aircraft with airspeed 650 km h^{-1} needs to travel in a direction of 028° when the wind is blowing from a direction of 139° at 80 km h^{-1}. Find, by using the sine rule in the vector triangle shown, the course to steer and the speed of the aircraft relative to the ground.

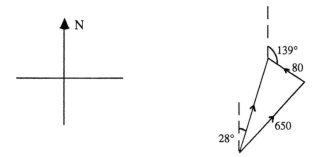

9 Repeat question 8 in the following cases. For each example, sketch the vector triangle.

(a) Airspeed = 830 km h^{-1}, direction of destination = 090°, wind speed = 70 km h^{-1}, wind blowing from 033°.

(b) Airspeed = 600 km h^{-1}, direction of destination = 248°, wind speed = 60 km h^{-1}, wind blowing from 107°.

Trigonometric identities

Some trigonometric formulas are very important because they are required in many different contexts. Among these are the **addition formulas** and the **double angle formulas**:

$\sin (A + B) = \sin A \cos B + \cos A \sin B$
$\sin (A - B) = \sin A \cos B - \cos A \sin B$
$\cos (A + B) = \cos A \cos B - \sin A \sin B$
$\cos (A - B) = \cos A \cos B + \sin A \sin B$

$\sin 2A = 2 \sin A \cos A$

$1 = \cos^2 A + \sin^2 A$

$\cos 2A = \cos^2 A - \sin^2 A$
$\quad\quad = 2 \cos^2 A - 1$
$\quad\quad = 1 - 2 \sin^2 A$

The following questions will help you to become familiar with these results.

1   (a)   Explain why the area of triangle OLM is $\frac{1}{2}pq \sin (A + B)$.

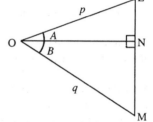

      (b)   Show that triangle OLN has area $\frac{1}{2}pq \sin A \cos B$.

      (c)   Find the area of triangle OMN in a similar form.

      (d)   Deduce that $\sin (A + B) = \sin A \cos B + \cos A \sin B$.

2   OFGH is a rhombus with side 1 unit.

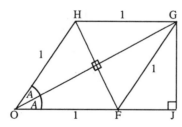

      (a)   Show that GJ = sin 2A and write down the length of FJ.

      (b)   Write down the lengths of OG, GJ, OJ, FJ in terms of sin A and cos A. What can you deduce about sin 2A and cos 2A?

3 Differentiate $\sin x \cos \alpha + \cos x \sin \alpha$ twice. (Treat α as a constant.) Comment on your result.

4 Use the product rule to differentiate $\sin x \cos x$, and the chain rule to differentiate $\sin^2 x$ and $\cos^2 x$. Comment on your results.

5 Sketch the graphs of $y = \sin x$ and $y = \sin^2 x$ on the same axes . Add the graphs of $y = \cos^2 x$, $y = \cos^2 x + \sin^2 x$ and $y = \cos^2 x - \sin^2 x$. Comment on your answers and confirm the results using a graph plotter.

6 Sketch the graphs of $y = \cos 2x$, $y = \cos 2x + 1$ and $y = \cos^2 x$ on the same axes. What relation do these graphs illustrate?

7 Use a graph plotter to draw the graphs of:

(a) $y = 2 \sin x \cos x$

(b) $y = \sin x \cos 0.5 - \cos x \sin 0.5$

(c) $y = \cos x \cos 0.5 + \sin x \sin 0.5$

8 Use trigonometric formulas to find:

(a) $\displaystyle\int_0^{\pi/2} \sin x \cos x \, dx$

(b) $\displaystyle\int_0^{\pi} \cos^2 x \, dx$

(c) $\displaystyle\int_0^{\pi/4} \sin^2 x \, dx$

Use graphs to provide rough checks of your answers.

9 Display the graphs of $y = 2 \sin 2x$ and $y = \cos x$ using a graph plotter. With the help of the double angle formulas, calculate (to 3 s.f.) the values of x between 0 and 2π at which the graphs meet.

10 Find all the values of x between 0 and 2π for which:

(a) $2 \cos 2x = 3 \cos x - 2$

(b) $\cos 2x = 3 \sin x$

11 Show that $\cos (A + B) + \cos(A - B) = 2 \cos A \cos B$, and use this result to find
$\displaystyle\int_0^{\pi/4} \cos 2x \cos x \, dx$ and $\displaystyle\int_0^{\pi/2} \cos 2x \cos x \, dx.$

12 Find the x-coordinates of the maximum and minimum points of $y = \cos 2x \cos x$ in the interval from 0 to 2π inclusive, by expressing $\frac{dy}{dx}$ in terms of $\sin x$ and $\cos x$. Use a graph plotter to give a rough check of your answers.

Further trigonometry

In this section there are some longer questions which make use of the double angle formulas:

$$\sin 2A = 2 \sin A \cos A$$
$$\cos 2A = 2 \cos^2 A - 1$$

and the Pythagoras relation: $1 = \cos^2 A + \sin^2 A$

1   A triangle has sides x, $\sqrt{x}$ and $1 - x$,
and its angles are α, β and γ as shown
in the diagram.

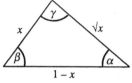

(a)   Use the cosine rule to find all the angles of the triangle when $x = 0.64$. What do you notice?

(b)   Explain why x cannot equal 0.2.

(c)   Show that $0.25 < x < 1$.

(d)   Show that $\cos \alpha = \dfrac{1}{2\sqrt{x}}$ and find $\cos \beta$ in terms of x.

(e)   Show that $\cos \beta = 2 \cos^2 \alpha - 1$.

(f)   Use the sine rule to show that $\sin \beta = 2 \sin \alpha \cos \alpha$.

(g)   What can you deduce from (e) and (f)?

2

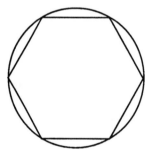 

The perimeter of a regular hexagon inscribed in a circle of radius 1 is not much less than the circumference of the circle. This is often used to demonstrate that $\pi \approx 3$.

The perimeter of a regular dodecahedron (12 sides) should give a better approximation and if you continue to double the number of sides the approximations should, theoretically, be increasingly accurate.

(a)   Show that the sides of the first three polygons are $2 \sin 30°$, $2 \sin 15°$ and $2 \sin 7.5°$.

(b)   Show that if X and x are the sides of two successive polygons of the sequence, then $X^2 = x^2 (4 - x^2)$.

(c)   From the relation in (b), obtain an expression for x in terms of X.

(d)   Show that the sequence of sides is given by $x_1 = 1$, $x_{i+1} = \sqrt{(2 - \sqrt{(4 - x_i^2)})}$.

(e)   Show that the sequence $3x_1$, $6x_2$, $12x_3$, ... converges to π.

(f)   Use one of the following programs and comment on the results.

CASIO	TEXAS
$1 \rightarrow X$	$1 \rightarrow X$
$3 \rightarrow M$	$3 \rightarrow M$
Lbl 1	Lbl A
$\sqrt{(2 - \sqrt{(4 - X^2)})} \rightarrow X$	$\sqrt{(2 - \sqrt{(4 - X^2)})} \rightarrow X$
$2M \rightarrow M$ ◢	$2M \rightarrow M$
$MX \rightarrow Y$ ◢	$M \times X \rightarrow Y$
Goto 1	Disp M
	Disp Y
	Pause
	Goto A

(g)   Change the first two instructions to $\sqrt{2} \rightarrow X$ and $2 \rightarrow M$, and run the program. Give a geometrical interpretation of the sequence.

3   You should have discovered that the rounding errors in the calculations of the sides of the polygons in question 2 become more and more serious as they are magnified by the increasing multiples. Therefore the method must be altered.

(a)   Show that $\sin 30° = \sin 15° \,(2 \cos 15°)$
$$= \sin 7.5° \,(2 \cos 15°)\,(2 \cos 7.5°)$$
$$= \sin 3.75° \,(2 \cos 15°)\,(2 \cos 7.5°)\,(2 \cos 3.75°)$$

(b)   Show that if $U = 2 \cos 2A$ and $u = 2 \cos A$, then $U = u^2 - 2$ and $u = \sqrt{(U + 2)}$.

(c)   Show that if $u_0 = \sqrt{3}$ and $u_{i+1} = \sqrt{(u_i + 2)}$, then 3, $\dfrac{6}{u_1}$, $\dfrac{12}{u_1 u_2}$, $\dfrac{24}{u_1 u_2 u_3}$, ... gives a sequence converging on π.

(d)   Use one of the following programs and comment on the results.

CASIO	TEXAS
$\sqrt{3} \rightarrow U$	$\sqrt{3} \rightarrow U$
$3 \rightarrow P$	$3 \rightarrow P$
Lbl 1	Lbl A
$\sqrt{(U + 2)} \rightarrow U$	$\sqrt{(U + 2)} \rightarrow U$
$2P \div U \rightarrow P$ ◢	$2P \div U \rightarrow P$
Goto 1	Disp P
	Pause
	Goto A

(e)   What initial values for U and P would correspond to the sequence of regular 4, 8, 16, 32, ... sided polygons? Use your calculator to confirm your answers.

Air resistance

In this exercise you will link various integration techniques and ideas concerning differential equations in the context of a small stone being thrown in the air.

1   A small stone is thrown vertically upwards with an initial speed of 6 ms⁻¹.

    (a)   Draw the velocity-time graph for the stone's upward journey.

    (b)   Neglecting air resistance, find how long the stone takes to reach its highest point and how high it rises.

Use the answers to question 1 to provide a rough check for the answers you obtain when air resistance which is proportional to the speed is introduced.

2   (a)   For question 1, explain why the upward velocity v at time t satisfies $\frac{dv}{dt} = -10$, and why the solution 'curve' has equation $v = -10t + 6$. (Assume the acceleration due to gravity is 10 ms⁻².)

    (b)   Interpret the differential equation $\frac{dv}{dt} = -10 - 0.4v$. If $v = 6$ when $t = 0$, what is the initial acceleration? What is the acceleration when the stone nears it highest point? Sketch the solution curve for the upward motion of the stone.

3   Carry out a step-by-step solution of the equation in question 2(b), with step $dt = 0.1$, for values of t up to 0.5. What time is suggested for the complete upward flight?

4   (a)   Show that the differential equation $\frac{dv}{dt} = -10 - 0.4v$ may be written:

$$\frac{dt}{dv} = -2.5 \times \frac{1}{25 + v}$$

    (b)   Integrate and use the initial values $v = 6$ when $t = 0$ to find the constant of integration. Hence find the total time for the upward motion. Explain why this is greater than the answer in question 3 but smaller than that in question 1.

5   (a)   Show that the solution in question 4 may be written in the form:

$$v = 31 \, e^{-0.4t} - 25$$

    (b)   Integrate this equation to find the greatest height reached.

6   Repeat the calculations of questions 4 and 5 with the slightly greater air resistance implied by the differential equation:

$$\frac{dv}{dt} = -10 - 0.5v$$

Keep the initial velocity as 6 ms⁻¹.

When looking at the motion of the stone as it descends, it is convenient to take the downwards direction as positive. With gravity accelerating the stone and air resistance opposing the stone's motion, the appropriate mathematical formulation might be:

$$\frac{dv}{dt} = 10 - 0.4v \text{ with } v = 0 \text{ when } t = 0$$

7 Carry out a step-by-step solution, with step $dt = 0.1$, for values of t up to 0.7.

8 Show that $t = -2.5 \ln(25 - v) + 2.5 \ln 25$. Find the time required for the speed to reach 6 ms^{-1}.

9 Rearrange the equation of question 8 in the form $v = f(t)$ and hence find v when $t = 0.5$. Integrate and show that the stone would need to fall about 2.15 m to attain a velocity of 6 ms^{-1}.

10 Show that a stone falling from rest from a great height with velocity subject to the differential equation:

$$\frac{dv}{dt} = 10 - 0.4v$$

would never travel faster than 25 ms^{-1} (known as the 'terminal velocity'). Sketch the solution curve. Find the terminal velocity of an object for which:

$$\frac{dv}{dt} = 10 - 0.5v$$

Tan and sec

Almost all trigonometric work can be carried out using only the sine and cosine functions. It is helpful, though, to know about the **tangent** and **secant** functions, which are defined by:

$$\tan x = \frac{\sin x}{\cos x} \quad \text{and} \quad \sec x = \frac{1}{\cos x}$$

The other two functions, the cotangent and cosecant functions, are less important and are omitted here.

When you use your calculator in later questions, make sure it is in radian mode.

1 Use the triangles below to write down the values of $\tan \frac{\pi}{4}$, $\sec \frac{\pi}{4}$, $\tan \frac{\pi}{4}$, $\tan \frac{\pi}{6}$, $\tan \frac{\pi}{3}$ and $\sec \frac{\pi}{3}$. Use a calculator to check your answers.

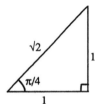 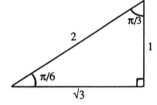

2 From the Pythagoras relation $\cos^2 x + \sin^2 x = 1$, deduce that:

$$1 + \tan^2 x = \sec^2 x$$

3 Use the quotient rule to show that differentiating $\tan x$ and $\sec x$ gives the following results.

y	$\frac{dy}{dx}$
$\tan x$	$\sec^2 x$
$\sec x$	$\sec x \tan x$

The tan and sec functions are closely interconnected. The following questions demonstrate this.

4 Differentiate $\ln (\sec x)$ and $\ln (\sec x + \tan x)$ using the chain rule and simplify the results. Use your results to complete the table.

y	$\int y \, dx$
	$\ln (\sec x) + c$
	$\ln (\sec x + \tan x) + c$

5   Sketch the graphs of $y = \tan x$ and $y = \sec x$. Check that they are consistent with previous results.

6   Find to 3 s.f. the gradients of:

(a) $y = \tan x$ at $x = \dfrac{\pi}{4}$

(b) $y = \sec x$ at $x = -\dfrac{\pi}{4}$

(c) $y = \sec x$ at $x = 0.9$

(d) $y = (\tan x)^2$ at $x = 1.3$ (use the chain rule)

(e) $y = \sec^2 x$ at $x = 1.3$

7   Evaluate the following to 3 s.f.

(a) $\displaystyle\int_0^{\pi/4} \sec^2 x \, dx$

(b) $\displaystyle\int_0^{\pi/4} \sec x \, dx$

(c) $\displaystyle\int_{-\pi/4}^{\pi/4} \tan x \, dx$

(d) $\displaystyle\int_0^{0.7} \tan x \, dx$

(e) $\displaystyle\int_{0.3}^{1.3} \sec x \tan x \, dx$

8   (a)   Use a graph plotter to draw the graph of $y = \tan^{-1} x$. How is this related to the graph of $y = \tan x$?

(b)   By writing $x = \tan y$ and showing that $\dfrac{dx}{dy} = 1 + x^2$ explain why the derivative of $\tan^{-1} x$ is $\dfrac{1}{1 + x^2}$.

9   Use the substitution $x = a \tan u$ to show that

$$\int \frac{1}{a^2 + x^2} \, dx = \frac{1}{a} \tan^{-1} \frac{x}{a} + c$$

10   Sketch the graph of $y = \dfrac{1}{1 + x^2}$. Find the approximate area under the graph from $x = 0$ to $x = 1$ using:

(a)   the trapezium rule with 2 strips;

(b)   the mid-ordinate rule with 2 strips.

Show that the correct area is $\dfrac{\pi}{4}$.

11   A stone is thrown vertically upwards at 8 ms^{-1}. The air resistance is proportional to v^2. While the stone is slowing down, its upward velocity v at time t is described by the differential equation:

$$\frac{dv}{dt} = -10 - 0.1 v^2$$

(a)   Sketch the solution curve and obtain a step-by-step solution, with step $dt = 0.1$, for values of t up to 0.6.

(b)   By first writing the equation as $\dfrac{dt}{dv} = \dfrac{-10}{100 + v^2}$, obtain t as a function of v and find how long the stone takes to reach its highest point.

(c)   Express v as a function of t and integrate to find the greatest height reached.

Calculus techniques

Differentiation is a straightforward mathematical operation. Apart from knowing the derivatives of the basic functions, you need only have the chain and product rules. Then you can cope with any combination of standard functions, however complicated, for example, $\sin^{-1}(e^{3x}\ln(2\sqrt{x}+5))$.

Integration is harder. You have a list of standard results and some techniques which are often helpful, for example, integration by substitution, integration by parts and partial fractions. However, many functions can only be integrated by a series of further techniques and there are still many which can only be integrated by approximate numerical means. This group of functions includes apparently simple ones such as e^{x^2} and $\dfrac{\sin x}{x}$.

1 Differentiate:

(a) $(3x+4)^5$
(b) $\sqrt{(3x+4)}$
(c) $(x^3+4)^5$
(d) $(\sqrt[3]{x}+4)^5$

(e) e^{3x}
(f) $\ln(3x+4)$
(g) $3\sin(4x+5)$
(h) $\cos(6\sqrt{x}+7)$

(i) $\sqrt{(\tan x)}$
(j) $\tan(\sqrt{x})$
(k) $\sqrt[3]{(x^2-4)}$
(l) $x(\sqrt{x}+8)$

(m) $x^2(e^{3x}+8)$
(n) $e^{x\ln x}$
(o) $\tan^{-1}\left(\dfrac{x}{6}\right)$
(p) $\sin^{-1}\left(\dfrac{x}{10}\right)$

2 Integrate the following. (Very little work is needed.)

(a) $(4x-1)^3$
(b) e^{4x-1}
(c) $9\cos(4x-1)$
(d) $x(4x-1)$

(e) $(4x-1)\sqrt{x}$
(f) $\sqrt{(4x-1)}$
(g) $x\sqrt{(4x^2-1)}$
(h) $(4x^2-1)^2$

(i) $\dfrac{1}{4x-1}$
(j) $\dfrac{1}{\sqrt{(4x-1)}}$
(k) $\dfrac{x}{3+x^2}$
(l) $\dfrac{x}{\sqrt{(3+x^2)}}$

(m) $\dfrac{6}{3+x^2}$
(n) $\dfrac{6}{\sqrt{(3-x^2)}}$
(o) $x\,e^{-\frac{1}{2}x^2}$

3 Use substitutions to find:

(a) $\displaystyle\int x\sqrt{(3x-2)}\,dx$ (let $u=3x-2$)
(b) $\displaystyle\int \dfrac{10}{\sqrt{x}+2}\,dx$ (let $u=\sqrt{x}+2$)

(c) $\displaystyle\int \dfrac{6}{4x^2+9}\,dx$ (let $x=\dfrac{3}{2}u$)
(d) $\displaystyle\int \dfrac{x-1}{(x+2)^2}\,dx$

(e) $\displaystyle\int \dfrac{e^x}{(e^x+3)^2}\,dx$
(f) $\displaystyle\int \dfrac{e^{2x}}{(e^x+3)^2}\,dx$

(g) $\displaystyle\int \dfrac{1}{\sqrt{(4+x^2)}}\,dx$ (let $x=2\tan u$)
(h) $\displaystyle\int \dfrac{1}{4-x^2}\,dx$ (let $x=2\sin u$)

4   Use integration by parts to find:

(a) $\int x\sqrt{(3x-2)}\,dx$ (b) $\int (x-1)(x+2)^{-2}\,dx$ (c) $\int x^2\,e^{5x}\,dx$ (d) $\int x\sin 3x\,dx$

(e) $\int x\sec^2 x\,dx$ (f) $\int (x+1)\sin^2 x\,dx$ (First use a trigonometric formula.)

5   Show that your answers (i) to questions 3(a) and 4(a), and (ii) to 3(d) and (4b), are equivalent. (iii) Check the answers to 3(b), (g) and (h) by differentiation.

6   Find $\int \ln x\,dx$ by using the substitution $u = \ln x$.

When an arc of a graph is rotated about the x-axis, the solid of revolution can be approximated by a collection of thin cylinders (one of which is indicated in the first diagram) and the volume is given exactly by $\int \pi y^2\,dx$. The 'dx' indicates that the y^2 must be replaced by the relevant function of x and the integration carried out in terms of x with the appropriate values of x as limits.

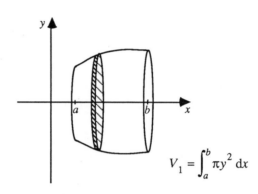

$$V_1 = \int_a^b \pi y^2\,dx$$

Similarly, a solid formed by revolution about the y-axis is given by $\int \pi x^2\,dy$.

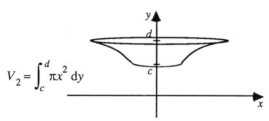

$$V_2 = \int_c^d \pi x^2\,dy$$

7   Find the volumes, V_1 and V_2, generated when the following arcs are rotated about the x-axis and about the y-axis, respectively.

(a) $y = \sqrt{x}$ from (0, 0) to (9, 3)   (b) $y = \sqrt{x} + 2$ from (1, 3) to (4, 4)

(c) $y = 3x$ from (0, 0) to (5, 15)   (d) $y = x^3 + 3$ from (0, 3) to (2, 11)

(e) $y = \left(\dfrac{h}{r}\right)x$ from (0, 0) to (r, h) (r and h are constants)

(f) $y = \sqrt{(r^2 - x^2)}$ from (0, r) to (r, 0)   (g) $y = \dfrac{1}{x}$ from $(\tfrac{1}{2}, 2)$ to $(2, \tfrac{1}{2})$

(h) $y = \dfrac{1}{\sqrt{x}}$ from (1, 1) to $(4, \tfrac{1}{2})$ (i) $y = e^x$ from (0, 1) to (1, e)

(j) $y = \cos x$ from (0, 1) to $(\tfrac{\pi}{2}, 0)$ (k) $y = \dfrac{x}{x+1}$ from (0, 0) to $(1, \tfrac{1}{2})$

8   Repeat question 7 for the following, using a numerical method (such as the mid-ordinate rule) whenever the integral is found to be too difficult or impossible.

(a) $y = e^{x^2}$ from (0, 1) to (1, e)   (b) $y = \sqrt{(\sin x)}$ from (0, 0) to $(\tfrac{\pi}{2}, 1)$

(c) $y = \dfrac{1}{\cos x}$ from (0, 1) to $(\tfrac{\pi}{3}, 2)$ (d) $y = \tan x$ from (0, 0) to $(\tfrac{\pi}{4}, 1)$

Polynomial approximations

For the following questions you will need to use the Maclaurin's series for various functions together with the Newton-Raphson process and the integrals:

$$\int \frac{1}{1+x^2} \, dx = \tan^{-1} x + c \quad \text{and} \quad \int \frac{1}{\sqrt{(1-x^2)}} \, dx = \sin^{-1} x + c$$

1.   Display together the graphs of $y = \ln(1+x)$ and $y = x$ and $y = x - \frac{x^2}{2}$ and $y = x - \frac{x^2}{2} + \frac{x^3}{3}$. Comment on your results.

2.   (a)   Replace x by $\sqrt{x}$ in the first three non-zero terms of the polynomial approximation for $\cos x$ and find values for $\cos \sqrt{0.2}$ and $\cos \sqrt{0.4}$. Compare your answers with the values given by your calculator.

   (b)   Use the approximation from (a) to find $\int_0^{0.4} \cos \sqrt{x} \, dx$. How accurate would you expect your answer to be?

3.   (a)   Find the first three non-zero terms of the approximation for $\sin^2 x$ by squaring the polynomial approximation for $\sin x$.

   (b)   Find the first four non-zero terms of the approximation for $\cos 2x$ by replacing x by $2x$ throughout.

   (c)   Explain the connection between your answers to (a) and (b).

4.   (a)   Write down polynomial approximations for $\ln(1+x^2)$ and $(1+x^2)^{-1}$, omitting terms involving x^{10} and higher powers.

   (b)   Differentiate the first polynomial in (a) and explain the connection with the second.

   (c)   Find $\int_0^{0.5} \ln(1+x^2) \, dx$ and $\int_0^{0.5} (1+x^2)^{-1} \, dx$ using the approximations.

   (d)   One of your answers to (c) can be checked easily. Check it.

5.   Find the following integrals using three non-zero terms of appropriate polynomial approximations in each case.

   (a) $\int_0^{0.6} x \cos x \, dx$ (b) $\int_{0.2}^{0.8} \frac{\sin x}{x} \, dx$ (c) $\int_0^{0.4} e^x \sin x \, dx$

   (d) $\int_0^{0.7} \sqrt{(1+x^4)} \, dx$ (e) $\int_{-0.4}^{0.4} \ln(1+x) \, dx$

   Check your answers by direct integration where possible. In (e), start by substituting $u = \ln(1+x)$.

6 Use **quadratic** polynomials to find approximate solutions of:

(a) $\cos x = 3x$ (b) $e^x = 2 - x$

Compare your answers with those given by the Newton-Raphson process.

7 (a) Write down the first four non-zero terms of the polynomial approximation for $e^{-\frac{1}{2}x^2}$.

(b) Display the graphs of $y = e^{-\frac{1}{2}x^2}$ and the polynomial from (a) simultaneously. For what values of x does the polynomial give a good fit to the exponential function?

(c) In probability theory, areas under the Normal curve $y = \frac{1}{\sqrt{(2\pi)}} e^{-\frac{1}{2}x^2}$ are important. Use one of the following programs with a variety of input values. Compare your results with answers found in probability tables.

CASIO

Lbl 1
? → X
$X - X^3 \div 6 + X^5 \div 40 - X^7 \div 336 \rightarrow Y$
$Y \div \sqrt{(2\pi)} + 0.5 \rightarrow Z$ ◢
Goto 1

TEXAS

Lbl 1
Input X
$X - X^3 \div 6 + X^5 \div 40 - X^7 \div 336 \rightarrow Y$
$Y \div \sqrt{(2\pi)} + 0.5 \rightarrow Z$
Disp Z
Goto 1

8 (a) Find the first four non-zero terms of polynomial approximations for $(1 - x^2)^{-\frac{1}{2}}$ and $\sin^{-1} x$. Hence find $\sin^{-1} 0.3$.

(b) Write down expressions for t_1, t_2, t_3 if $t_0 = x$, $t_1 = t_0 \times \frac{1}{2} x^2 \div 1$, $t_2 = t_1 \times \frac{3}{2} x^2 \div 2$ and $t_3 = t_2 \times \frac{5}{2} x^2 \div 3$. Show that the first four terms of the series for $\sin^{-1}x$ are then t_0, $t_1 \div 3$, $t_2 \div 5$ and $t_3 \div 7$.

(c) Use one of the following programs to find $\sin^{-1} 0.3$. How many terms are needed to achieve 8 s.f. accuracy?

CASIO

? → X
X → T: X → S: X² → U
1 → M: 3 → D
Lbl 1
T x (M − 0.5) x U ÷ M → T
S + T ÷ D → S ◢
M + 1 → M: D + 2 → D
Goto 1

TEXAS

Input X
X → T
X → S
X² → U
1 → M
3 → D
Lbl 1
T x (M − 0.5) x U ÷ M → T
S + T ÷ D → S
Disp S
M + 1 → M
D + 2 → D
Goto 1

(d) Find $\sin^{-1} 0.5$ to 8 s.f. Multiply your answer by 6 and comment.

9 Find polynomial approximations for $(1 + x^2)^{-1}$ and $\tan^{-1}x$. Write and use a program to evaluate $\tan^{-1}x$.

SOLUTIONS

Sigma notation and series

This exercise uses the general result

$$\sum_{1}^{n} \left[\, f(i+1) - f(i) \,\right] \;=\; f(n+1) - f(1)$$

to derive the following useful formulas.

$$\sum_{1}^{n} i \;=\; \tfrac{1}{2} n(n+1)$$

$$\sum_{1}^{n} i(i+1) \;=\; \tfrac{1}{3} n(n+1)(n+2)$$

$$\sum_{1}^{n} i(i+1)(i+2) \;=\; \tfrac{1}{4} n(n+1)(n+2)(n+3)$$

This pattern can be extended.

$$\sum_{1}^{n} i^{2} \;=\; \tfrac{1}{6} n(n+1)(2n+1)$$

$$\sum_{1}^{n} i^{3} \;=\; \tfrac{1}{4} n^{2}(n+1)^{2}$$

1 $(\sqrt{2}-1) + (\sqrt{3}-\sqrt{2}) + (\sqrt{4}-\sqrt{3}) + (\sqrt{5}-\sqrt{4}) = \sqrt{5}-1$

$$\sum_{1}^{5} \left[(i+1)^{2} - i^{2} \right] = 6^{2} - 1^{2} \quad \text{and more generally} \quad \sum_{1}^{n} \left[f(i+1) - f(i) \right] = f(n+1) - f(1)$$

for any function f, the intermediate terms cancelling as in the first example.

2 $\displaystyle\sum_{1}^{n} (2i+1) = \sum_{1}^{n} \left[(i+1)^{2} - i^{2} \right] = (n+1)^{2} - 1; \quad 3+5+7 = 15 = 4^{2} - 1$

3 $\displaystyle\sum_{1}^{n} (2i-1) = \sum_{1}^{n} \left[i^{2} - (i-1)^{2} \right] = n^{2} - 0^{2} = n^{2}$

The i-th L-shaped plot contains $(2i-1)$ symbols; the first n plots together contain n^2 symbols.

4 $2\sum_{1}^{n} i = \sum_{1}^{n} \left[i(i+1) - i(i-1) \right] = n(n+1) - 0.$ Hence $\sum_{1}^{n} i = \frac{1}{2} n(n+1).$

5 $f(i+1) - f(i) = i(i+1)(i+2) - (i-1)i(i+1) = i(i+1)\left[(i+2) - (i-1)\right] = 3i(i+1).$

So $\sum_{1}^{n} i(i+1) = \frac{1}{3}\left[f(n+1) - f(1) \right] = \frac{1}{3} n(n+1)(n+2)$

6 Take $f(x) = (x-1)x(x+1)(x+2).$

7 The missing expression is $\frac{1}{6} n(n+1)\left[2(n+2) - 3 \right]$

8 $\sum_{1}^{4} (i-1)i(i+1) = 0 + 1 \times 2 \times 3 + 2 \times 3 \times 4 + 3 \times 4 \times 5 = \sum_{1}^{3} i(i+1)(i+2)$

The sum of n terms is the formula of question 6 with n replaced by $(n-1).$

Now $(i-1)i(i+1) = i^{3} - i,$

so $\sum_{1}^{n} i^{3} = \sum_{1}^{n}\left[(i-1)i(i+1) + i \right] = \frac{1}{4}(n-1)n(n+1)(n+2) + \frac{1}{2} n(n+1)$

$$= \frac{1}{4} n(n+1)\left[(n-1)(n+2) + 2 \right]$$

$$= \frac{1}{4} n(n+1)(n^{2}+n)$$

$$= \frac{1}{4} n^{2}(n+1)^{2}$$

Any polynomial in i can be expressed as a combination of multiples of $i,$ $i(i+1),$
$i(i+1)(i+2)$ and so on, and a formula for the sum of n terms follows. A further example
is provided by question 10.

9 $\displaystyle\sum_1^n (3i^2 + 3i + 1) = \sum_1^n \left[(i+1)^3 - i^3 \right] = (n+1)^3 - 1$

Hence $\displaystyle 3\sum_1^n i^2 + 3\sum_1^n i + n = n^3 + 3n^2 + 3n$

$$\sum_1^n i^2 = \frac{1}{3}\left[n^3 + 3n^2 + 3n - \frac{3}{2}n(n+1) - n \right]$$

$$= \frac{1}{3}\left[n^3 + 3n^2 + 2n - \frac{3}{2}n(n+1) \right]$$

$$= \frac{1}{3}\left[n(n+1)(n+2) - \frac{3}{2}n(n+1) \right]$$

$$= \frac{1}{6}n(n+1)\left[2(n+2) - 3 \right]$$

$$= \frac{1}{6}n(n+1)(2n+1)$$

10 $(i-1)\,i\,(i+1)(i+2) = (i^3 - i)(i+2) = i^4 + 2i^3 - i^2 - 2i$

So $\quad i^4 = (i-1)\,i\,(i+1)(i+2) - 2i^3 + i^2 + 2i$

$\quad = (i-1)\,i\,(i+1)(i+2) - 2(i-1)\,i\,(i+1) + i^2$

and $\displaystyle \sum_1^n i^4 = \frac{1}{5}(n-1)\,n\,(n+1)(n+2)(n+3) - \frac{1}{2}(n-1)\,n\,(n+1)(n+2)$

$$+ \frac{1}{6}n(n+1)(2n+1)$$

Checks: $\quad n = 2:\qquad 1 + 16 = 24 - 12 + 5$

$\quad\quad\quad\quad n = 3:\qquad 1 + 16 + 81 = 144 - 60 + 14$

11 (a) $\displaystyle \sum_1^n i^2$ is an integer so $\frac{1}{6}n(n+1)(2n+1)$ is an integer,

i.e. $n(n+1)(2n+1)$ is divisible by 6.

(b) n, $n+1$ are consecutive integers, so one of them is divisible by 2. In any set of three consecutive integers, one must be divisible by 3. Either n or $n+1$ is divisible by 3, or both $n-1$ and $n+2$ are divisible by 3.

In this last case, $(n-1) + (n+2) = 2n+1$ is also divisible by 3.
Hence $n(n+1)(2n+1)$ is divisible by 2 and by 3, and therefore by 6.

36

12 (a) $S = \displaystyle\sum_{n+1}^{2n} i^2 = \sum_{1}^{2n} i^2 - \sum_{1}^{n} i^2 = \frac{1}{6}(2n)(2n+1)(4n+1) - \frac{1}{6}n(n+1)(2n+1)$

$$= \frac{1}{6}n(2n+1)(8n+2-n-1)$$

$$= \frac{1}{6}n(2n+1)(7n+1)$$

Check: For $n = 2$, $S = 9 + 16 = 25$; $\frac{1}{6}n(2n+1)(7n+1) = \frac{1}{6} \times 2 \times 5 \times 15 = 25$

(b) $\displaystyle\sum_{n}^{2n} i^3 = \sum_{1}^{2n} i^3 - \sum_{1}^{n-1} i^3 = \frac{1}{4}(2n)^2(2n+1)^2 - \frac{1}{4}(n-1)^2 n^2$

$$= \frac{1}{4}n^2\left[4(2n+1)^2 - (n-1)^2\right]$$

$$= \frac{1}{4}n^2\left[2(2n+1) - (n-1)\right]\left[2(2n+1) + (n-1)\right]$$

$$= \frac{1}{4}n^2(3n+3)(5n+1)$$

$$= \frac{3}{4}n^2(n+1)(5n+1)$$

$n = 2$ gives $8 + 27 + 64 = 99$ and $\frac{3}{4} \times 4 \times 3 \times 11 = 99$

13 (a) $S_1 = \displaystyle\sum_{1}^{n}(2i-1)^2 = \sum_{1}^{n}(4i^2 - 4i + 1)$

$$= \frac{2}{3}n(n+1)(2n+1) - 2n(n+1) + n$$

$$= \frac{2}{3}n(n+1)(2n+1) - (2n^2 + n)$$

$$= \frac{1}{3}n(2n+1)(2n+2-3) = \frac{1}{3}n(2n+1)(2n-1)$$

(b) $S_2 = \displaystyle\sum_{1}^{n}(2i)^2 = 4\sum_{1}^{n} i^2 = \frac{2}{3}n(n+1)(2n+1)$

$S_1 + S_2 = \frac{1}{3}n(2n+1)(2n-1+2n+2) = \frac{1}{6}(2n)(2n+1)(4n+1) = \displaystyle\sum_{1}^{2n} i^2$

14 $S_1 = \frac{1}{2}$, $S_2 = \frac{2}{3}$, $S_3 = \frac{3}{4}$, $S_4 = \frac{4}{5}$ suggesting $S_n = \frac{n}{n+1}$.

$\dfrac{x}{x+1} - \dfrac{x-1}{x} = \dfrac{1}{x(x+1)}$ so $\displaystyle\sum_{1}^{n} \dfrac{1}{i(i+1)} = f(n+1) - f(1)$ where $f(x) = \dfrac{x-1}{x}$

$$= \frac{n}{n+1}$$

Maximum and minimum points

1   (a) $(1.5, 30.25)$ (b) $(0, 0)$ and $(3.3, -18.5)$

    (c) $(5, 0)$ and $(1.7, 18.5)$ (d) $(4, 0)$ and $(0.7, 18.5)$

    Note that (c) is a $180°$ rotation of (b), while (d) is a translation of (c).

    (e) $(2.1, -6.0)$ and $(-2.1, 30.0)$ (f) $(-0.1, 6.0)$ and $(4.1, -30.0)$

    Notice also the connection between the graphs of (e) and (f).

2   (a) $y = 0$ when $2x + 3 = 0$ or $x - 5 = 0$
                          $x = -1.5$ or 5

        The graph of every quadratic function is symmetrical, so the x-coordinate of the minimum point is $\frac{1}{2}(-1.5 + 5) = 1.75$.

        Multiplying out the brackets and differentiating gives the same answer.

               $y = 2x^2 - 7x - 15$

        $\Rightarrow$ $\dfrac{dy}{dx} = 4x - 7$
                      $= 0$ when $x = 1.75$

        Then $y = -21.1$

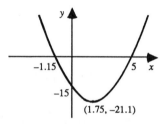

    (b)

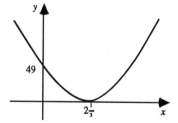

                              No differentiation is required here.

    (c)   Because the $(2x - 9)$ bracket is squared in the expression for y, the graph touches the x-axis at $(4.5, 0)$. You can see that $y = 0$ when $x = 4.5$ and $y > 0$ if x is just less than 4.5 and also if x is just greater than 4.5.

        The sketch graph shows that the expression for $\dfrac{dy}{dx}$ must have $(2x - 9)$ as one factor.

               $y = 4x^3 - 36x^2 + 81x$

               gives $\dfrac{dy}{dx} = 3(2x - 9)(2x - 3)$

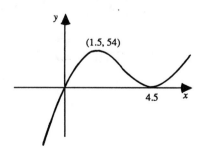

(d) This time $\frac{dy}{dx}$ does not factorise, so you must use the quadratic equation formula to find the x-coordinates of the maximum and minimum points.

$$y = x^3 - 6x^2 - x + 30$$

gives $\frac{dy}{dx} = 3x^2 - 12x - 1$

$\qquad = 0$ when $x = \frac{12 \pm \sqrt{156}}{6}$

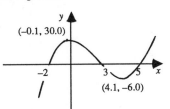

Compare with question 1(e).

(e) $\qquad y = 4x^3 - 4x^2 - 3x$

gives $\frac{dy}{dx} = 12x^2 - 8x - 3$

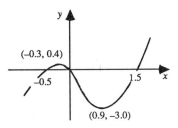

3 The first graph crosses the x-axis at one point; the second crosses it at three points.

(a) 3 $\qquad$ (b) 2 $\qquad$ (c) 1

4 (a) $(2, -9), (-2, 23)$ $\qquad$ (b) $(2, -33), (-2, -1)$ $\qquad$ (c) None

(d) 3 $\qquad$ (e) 1 $\qquad$ (f) 1

5 For the graph of $y = x^3 - ax + b$, you require a maximum and a minimum point, with the y-coordinate of the maximum point positive and the y-coordinate of the minimum point negative.

$$3x^2 - a = 0 \quad \text{when} \quad x = \pm \sqrt{\left(\frac{a}{3}\right)} \text{ provided } a \geq 0$$

When $\quad x = \sqrt{\left(\frac{a}{3}\right)}, \quad y = -\frac{2}{3}a\sqrt{\left(\frac{a}{3}\right)} + b$

When $\quad x = -\sqrt{\left(\frac{a}{3}\right)}, \quad y = \frac{2}{3}a\sqrt{\left(\frac{a}{3}\right)} + b$

You require $-\frac{2}{3}a\sqrt{\left(\frac{a}{3}\right)} < b < \frac{2}{3}a\sqrt{\left(\frac{a}{3}\right)}$,

i.e. $b^2 < \left[\frac{2}{3}a\sqrt{\left(\frac{a}{3}\right)}\right]^2 = \frac{4a^3}{27}$

Real values of b satisfying this condition can only be found if $a > 0$.

6 $y = \sqrt{x}$ implies $y^2 = x$. This is the equation $y = x^2$ with the roles of x and y interchanged. So the graph of $y^2 = x$ is that of $y = x^2$ reflected in the line $y = x$. But the graph of $y = \sqrt{x}$ is only the top half of $y^2 = x$ because of the definition of the square root function.

$$y = x^2 \text{ implies } \frac{dy}{dx} = 2x \text{ so the gradient at Q is } 2\sqrt{a}.$$

The gradient at P is therefore $\frac{1}{2\sqrt{a}}$, hence the derivative of $\sqrt{x}$ is $\frac{1}{2\sqrt{x}}$.

7　(a)　$\frac{dy}{dx} = 1 - \frac{1}{2\sqrt{x}}$

　　　　$= 0$ when $x = \frac{1}{4}$, $y = -\frac{1}{4}$.

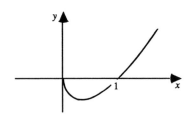

(b)　This graph is an enlargement of that in (a) with scale factor 100.

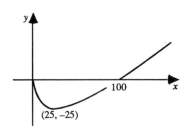

$(25, -25)$

(c)　There are no maximum or minimum points.

　　　If you attempt to solve $1 + \frac{1}{2\sqrt{x}} = 0$,

　　　you obtain $\sqrt{x} = -\frac{1}{2}$ which is impossible.

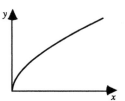

(d)　$\frac{dy}{dx} = 2x - \frac{4}{\sqrt{x}} = 0$ when $x\sqrt{x} = 2 \Rightarrow (\sqrt{x})^3 = 2 \Rightarrow x = (\sqrt[3]{2})^2 \approx 1.6$

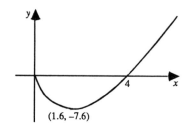

$(1.6, -7.6)$

8　The graph of $y = x^3$ has gradient $3(\sqrt[3]{a})^2$ at $(\sqrt[3]{a}, a)$, so the graph of $y = \sqrt[3]{x}$ has gradient $\frac{1}{3(\sqrt[3]{a})^2}$ where $x = a$.

　Consequently $y = \sqrt[3]{x} \Rightarrow \frac{dy}{dx} = \frac{1}{3(\sqrt[3]{x})^2}$

9　(a)　From the intersections with the x-axis, the equation must have the form
　　　$y = k(x + 2)(x - 3)(x - 5)$. Putting $x = 0$ gives $k = \frac{1}{10}$.

(b)　$y = kx(x - 6)^2$ where $16 = k \times 2 \times 16$, giving $k = \frac{1}{2}$.

　　　You can check that $\frac{dy}{dx} = 0$ when $x = 2$.

(c) $\frac{dy}{dx} = k (x + 3) (x - 3)$ for some k,

$\qquad = k (x^2 - 9)$

Integrating gives $y = k (\frac{1}{3} x^3 - 9x)$, with no constant term since $y = 0$ when $x = 0$.

Also $-5 = k (9 - 27)$, so $k = \frac{5}{18}$.

(d) $\frac{dy}{dx} = k x (x - 4) = k (x^2 - 4x)$

$\quad y = k (\frac{1}{3} x^3 - 2x^2) + 3$, remembering that $y = 3$ when $x = 0$.

Putting $x = 4$ and $y = -3$ gives $k = \frac{9}{16}$.

(e) $\frac{dy}{dx} = k (x +1) (x - 3) = k (x^2 - 2x - 3)$

$\Rightarrow y = k (\frac{1}{3} x^3 - x^2 - 3x) + l$

The coordinates of the maximum and minimum points now give simultaneous equations:

$$-8 = \frac{5}{3} k + l, \quad 24 = -9k + l$$

with solutions $k = -3$, $l = -3$.

The final equation is $y = -x^3 + 3x^2 + 9x - 3$.

10   The equation has the form $y = kx^2 (x - a)$ where k and a are constants. Differentiation then gives the x-coordinate of the maximum point as $\frac{2}{3} a$.

If you write $a = 3b$, you then need to calculate

$$k \int_0^{2b} x^2 (x - 3b)\, dx \text{ and } k \int_{2b}^{3b} x^2 (x - 3b)\, dx, \text{ giving } -4kb^4 \text{ and } -\frac{11}{4} kb^4. \; k \text{ is negative and the}$$

required ratio is $4 : \frac{11}{4} = 16 : 11$.

Parabolic and elliptical reflectors

1   When $x = 6$, $y = 9$ and $\frac{dy}{dx} = \frac{1}{2} x = 3$. FP $= \sqrt{(6^2 + (9 - 1)^2)} = 10$

The dotted lines have length 6 and 18 (because of the gradient) and so FQ $= 18 - 9 + 1 = 10$.

FP $=$ FQ $\Rightarrow \alpha = \gamma$ so $\beta = \gamma$ and PR is parallel to the y-axis.

2 (a) When $x = 10$, $y = 25$, $\frac{dy}{dx} = 5$, FP $= 26$, FQ $= 26$

(b) When $x = 4$, $y = 4$, $\frac{dy}{dx} = 2$, FP $= 5$, FQ $= 5$

(c) When $x = 2$, $y = 1$, $\frac{dy}{dx} = 1$, FP $= 2$, FQ $= 2$

When $x = t$, $y = \frac{1}{4}t^2$, $\frac{dy}{dx} = \frac{1}{2}t$;

then FP $= \sqrt{(t^2 + (\frac{1}{4}t^2 - 1)^2)} = \sqrt{(\frac{1}{16}t^4 + \frac{1}{2}t^2 + 1)} = \frac{1}{4}t^2 + 1$

Q is $t \times \frac{1}{2}t = \frac{1}{2}t^2$ below P and FQ $= \frac{1}{2}t^2 - \frac{1}{4}t^2 + 1 = \frac{1}{4}t^2 + 1$

In each case it follows that $\alpha = \beta = \gamma$ and the reflected ray is parallel to the y-axis.

3 The parabola must have gradient 1 at S.

(a) For $y = x^2$, the gradient $2x$ equals 1 at the point $(\frac{1}{2}, \frac{1}{4})$, so G must be $(0, \frac{1}{4})$.

Then if P is (t, t^2), then GP $= \sqrt{(t^2 + (t^2 - \frac{1}{4})^2)} = t^2 + \frac{1}{4}$.

Also GQ $= t \times 2t - t^2 + \frac{1}{4} = t^2 + \frac{1}{4}$ and the light property follows.

(b) For $y = 3x^2$, S is $(\frac{1}{6}, \frac{1}{12})$ and G must be $(0, \frac{1}{12})$.

Then if P is $(t, 3t^2)$, you will find that GP $=$ GQ $= 3t^2 + \frac{1}{12}$.

4 For $y = kx^2$, the focus must be $(0, \frac{1}{4k})$ and GP $=$ GQ $= kt^2 + \frac{1}{4k}$, which fits with all the previous findings.

5 For $16x^2 + 25y^2 = 400$, $y = 0$ gives $x = \pm 5$ while $x = 0$ gives $y = \pm 4$;

A is therefore $(5, 0)$ and B is $(0, 4)$.

Since C is $(0, 5)$, the scale factor of the stretch is $\frac{4}{5} = 0.8$.

OU has gradient $\frac{3}{4}$. The tangent at U is perpendicular to OU so it has gradient $-\frac{4}{3}$.

V is $(4, 3 \times \frac{4}{5}) = (4, 2.4)$ and the gradient at V is $-\frac{4}{3} \times \frac{4}{5} = -\frac{16}{15}$ because the stretch affects the gradient in the same way as it affects y-coordinates.

$\alpha = \tan^{-1}\left(\frac{2.4}{4-3}\right) \approx 67.4°$ $\beta = \tan^{-1}\left(\frac{2.4}{4+3}\right) \approx 18.9°$

$\gamma = 180° + \tan^{-1}\left(-\frac{16}{15}\right) \approx 133.2°$ $\delta = \gamma - \alpha \approx 65.8°$

$\varepsilon = 180° - (\gamma - \beta) \approx 65.7°$

$\delta \approx \varepsilon$ implies that a ray of light along FV will be reflected along VF′, i.e. through F′.

FV $= \sqrt{(1^2 + 2.4^2)} = 2.6$ F′V $= \sqrt{(7^2 + 2.4^2)} = 7.4$

6

x-coordinate of U	U	V	Gradient at V	δ	ε	FV	F'V
1	$(1, \sqrt{24})$	$(1, 3.92)$	-0.163	$53.7°$	$53.7°$	4.4	5.6
2	$(2, \sqrt{21})$	$(2, 3.67)$	-0.349	$55.6°$	$55.5°$	3.8	6.2
3	$(3, 4)$	$(3, 3.2)$	-0.6	$59.0°$	$59.1°$	3.2	6.8
4	$(4, 3)$	$(4, 2.4)$	-1.067	$65.8°$	$65.7°$	2.6	7.4

$\delta \approx \varepsilon$ in each case, confirming the light property of the ellipse. $FV + F'V = 10$, as will be proved in question 7.

7 The y-coordinate of V is $0.8\sqrt{(25 - t^2)}$.

$FV = \sqrt{[0.8^2(25 - t^2) + (t - 3)^2]} = \sqrt{(25 - 6t + 0.36t^2)} = 5 - 0.6t$.
Similarly, $F'V = 5 + 0.6t$.

For the general ellipse, $FV = \sqrt{\left[\dfrac{a^2b^2 - b^2t^2}{a^2} + (t - c)^2\right]}$

$\qquad = \dfrac{1}{a}\sqrt{(a^2b^2 - b^2t^2 + a^2t^2 - 2a^2ct + a^2c^2)}$

$\qquad = \dfrac{1}{a}\sqrt{(a^4 - 2a^2ct + c^2t^2)} = \dfrac{1}{a}(a^2 - ct) = a - \dfrac{ct}{a}$

Similarly, $F'V = a + \dfrac{ct}{a}$ so that $FV + F'V = 2a$.

In questions 5, 6, 7 you start with an ellipse as a squashed circle, then discover that $FV + F'V$ is the same for all positions of V. This fact could be used as the starting point.

8 Using a ruler and compasses, many points on the locus of P can be constructed such that $AP + BP = k$, a constant (with fixed points A and B). For example, with $AB = 6$ cm, $k = 10$ cm, giving the points on the diagram as shown in the table.

AP	8 cm	7 cm	6 cm	5 cm
BP	2 cm	3 cm	4 cm	5 cm
	P_1	P_2 and P_3	P_4 and P_5	P_6 and P_7

Joining up the points gives the ellipse. Different shapes and sizes can be produced by taking different values for the lengths AB and k. Question 7 explains why this locus is an ellipse.

A more dramatic (though less accurate) way of producing the locus is to fasten a piece of paper to a drawing board with two drawing pins close to the centre of the paper. A loop of string or thread is then placed round the pins and pulled tight with a pencil as shown. Moving the pencil once round the pins while keeping the string taut gives the ellipse.

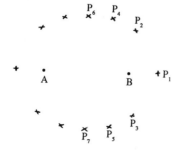
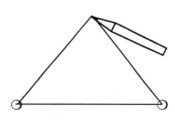

Solving equations

1 (a) 2 (b) 1.95 (c) 141 (d) 1.56

(e) 27.9 (f) 0.519 (g) No answer; $\sin^{-1}x$ lies between $-\frac{1}{2}\pi$ and $\frac{1}{2}\pi$.

(h) 0.460, 2.68, 6.74, 8.96

2 (a) 9.84 (b) 0.229 (c) 3.65

(d) −0.111 (e) ±0.168

3 (a) $x = 2\left[\left(\frac{y}{7}\right)^2 - 3\right] = \frac{2y^2}{49} - 6$ (b) $x = \frac{1}{2}(10^{y/4} - 1)$

(c) $x = \frac{1}{4}\ln\left(\frac{y}{5}\right)$ (d) $x = \frac{1}{8}e^{(y-6)/2}$

4 This equation cannot be solved algebraically, nor can most of those in later questions of this exercise but solutions to any desired accuracy can always be obtained by iterative methods.

0, 1, 0.5, 0.707, 0.613, 0.654,

0.635, 0.644, 0.640, 0.642,

0.641, 0.641

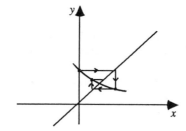

5 (a) 4.54 (b) 1.25 (c) 1.93 (d) 0.631

6 $x = \dfrac{\log 2}{\log 3} = \dfrac{\ln 2}{\ln 3} = 0.631$

The sequence starts 1, 2, 9, 19690 and clearly diverges. The gradient of the graph of $y = x + 3^x - 2$ is about 1.7 where it crosses $y = x$. The sequence diverges because this gradient is greater than 1.

7

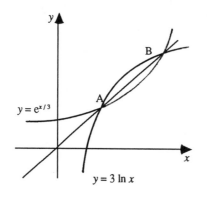

Notice again that the graphs of a function and its inverse are reflections of each other in $y = x$. They must therefore cross $y = x$ at the same points. If one graph is steep at such a point, the other is shallow. When an iterative sequence given by $x_{i+1} = f(x_i)$ converges, the graph of $y = f(x)$ at the relevant point must have gradient between −1 and 1.

44

This explains why the sequence of question 5(a) converges on B, where the gradient of $y = 3 \ln x$ is less than 1.

$x = 3 \ln x \Rightarrow e^{x/3} = x$, and whatever the starting value, the iteration $x_{i+1} = e^{x_i/3}$ converges on the x-coordinate of A, which is 1.86 to 3 significant figures.

8 $x_{i+1} = e^{x_i} - 2$ gives the solution -1.84.

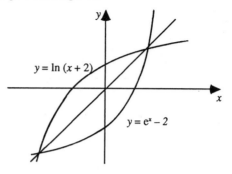

$x_{i+1} = \ln (x_i + 2)$ gives the solution 1.15.

9   The maximum and minimum points of $y = x^3 - 3x + 1$ are $(-1, 3)$ and $(1, -1)$. The roots are roughly -2, 0.5 and 1.5.

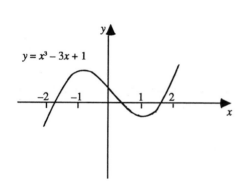

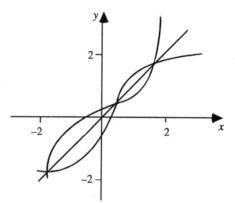

$f^{-1}(x) = \sqrt[3]{(3x - 1)}$

$x_{i+1} = f(x_i)$ gives the root 0.34730.

$x_{i+1} = f^{-1}(x_i)$ gives 1.5321 and -1.8794.

Note that the sum of the three roots is zero.

10   (a)   If OB $= 3$ cm, BD $=$ BE $= (3 - \frac{1}{2}d)$ cm, AD $=$ AC $= (4 - \frac{1}{2}d)$ cm and $(3 - \frac{1}{2}d) + (4 - \frac{1}{2}d) = 5$, giving $d = 2$.

       BN $= (3 - x)$ cm, so similar triangles give $\frac{3-x}{x} = \frac{3}{4}$, from which $x = \frac{12}{7}$.

       BA $=$ BR $+$ RQ $+$ QA $= \frac{3}{4}y + y + \frac{4}{3}y = 5$, giving $y = \frac{60}{37}$.

       Note that $d > x > y$.

       The required areas are π, 2.94 and 2.63 cm².

(b)　The method used in (a) gives $d = h (\sin \theta + \cos \theta - 1)$.

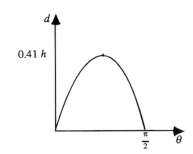

The graph is clearly symmetrical because of the situation from which it arises or, more formally, from the transformation $\theta \to \frac{\pi}{2} - \theta$ which leaves d unchanged. The same applies to the graphs of (c) and (d).

When $\theta = \frac{\pi}{4}$, $d = (\sqrt{2} - 1) h \approx 0.41h$

The gradient formula is $h (\cos \theta - \sin \theta) = h$ when $\theta = 0$.

(c)　$\dfrac{h \sin \theta - x}{x} = \dfrac{h \sin \theta}{h \cos \theta}$ gives $x = \dfrac{h \sin \theta \cos \theta}{\sin \theta + \cos \theta}$

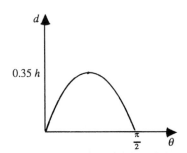

When $\theta = \dfrac{\pi}{4}$, $x = \dfrac{\sqrt{2}h}{4} \approx 0.35h$

$\dfrac{x}{\theta} = \left(\dfrac{h \cos \theta}{\sin \theta + \cos \theta} \right) \times \left(\dfrac{\sin \theta}{\theta} \right)$

As θ tends to 0, $\dfrac{x}{\theta}$ tends to $h \times 1 = h$, so the gradient at the origin is the same as in (b). Notice that this gradient can be found without attempting to obtain the derived function, a task requiring techniques from later units.

(d)　$\left(\dfrac{\sin \theta}{\cos \theta} + 1 + \dfrac{\cos \theta}{\sin \theta} \right) y = h$, and hence

$y = \dfrac{h \sin \theta \cos \theta}{(\sin \theta)^2 + (\cos \theta)^2 + \sin \theta \cos \theta}$

$= \dfrac{h \sin \theta \cos \theta}{1 + \sin \theta \cos \theta}$ using the trigonometric form of Pythagoras.

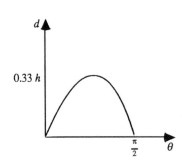

When $\theta = \dfrac{\pi}{4}$, $y = \dfrac{1}{3} h \approx 0.33h$

$\dfrac{y}{\theta} = \left(\dfrac{h \cos \theta}{1 + \sin \theta \cos \theta} \right) \times \left(\dfrac{\sin \theta}{\theta} \right) \to h$ as $\theta \to 0$

The three graphs look much the same and have the same gradient at the origin. The maximum points are at slightly different heights.

(e) For $0 < \theta < \frac{\pi}{2}$,

$$x > y \Leftrightarrow \sin \theta + \cos \theta < 1 + \sin \theta \cos \theta$$

$$\Leftrightarrow 0 < 1 - \sin \theta - \cos \theta + \sin \theta \cos \theta$$

$$\Leftrightarrow 0 < (1 - \sin \theta)(1 - \cos \theta)$$

Now $\sin \theta < 1$ and $\cos \theta < 1$, so $(1 - \sin \theta)(1 - \cos \theta) > 0$.

Since the implication symbols are used correctly above, it follows that $x > y$ for all θ between 0 and $\frac{\pi}{2}$.

(f) $d > x \Leftrightarrow \sin \theta + \cos \theta - 1 > \dfrac{\sin \theta \cos \theta}{\sin \theta + \cos \theta}$

$$\Leftrightarrow (\sin \theta + \cos \theta)^2 - \sin \theta - \cos \theta > \sin \theta \cos \theta$$

$$\Leftrightarrow 1 + 2 \sin \theta \cos \theta - \sin \theta - \cos \theta - \sin \theta \cos \theta > 0$$

$$\Leftrightarrow 1 - \sin \theta - \cos \theta + \sin \theta \cos \theta > 0$$

$$\Leftrightarrow (1 - \sin \theta)(1 - \cos \theta) > 0$$

The proof is completed exactly as in (e).

(g) No. For small θ, both d and x are approximately equal to θh.

Hence $\frac{1}{4} \pi d^2 < x^2$.

As a supplementary question, you might like to find, by decimal search, the values of θ for which the areas are the same.

Adding vectors

1 $\begin{bmatrix} 5 \\ 3 \end{bmatrix}$ $r = \sqrt{(25 + 9)} = 5.83$, $\theta = \tan^{-1}\left(\frac{3}{5}\right) = 31.0°$

(a) 5.8 at $59.0° = 90° - 31.0°$ (b) 10 at $90°$ (c) 12.5 at $151.4°$

(d) 12.5 at $-28.6°$ (opposite to (c))   (e) 5 at $-126.9°$

Negative angles imply a clockwise rotation from the x-direction.

2 (a) $\begin{bmatrix} 2.3 \\ 1.6 \end{bmatrix}$ (b) $\begin{bmatrix} -7.3 \\ 0 \end{bmatrix}$ (c) $\begin{bmatrix} -15.9 \\ 8.5 \end{bmatrix}$ (d) $\begin{bmatrix} 15.9 \\ -8.5 \end{bmatrix}$

(e) Same as (d)   (f) $\begin{bmatrix} -17.7 \\ -17.7 \end{bmatrix}$ (g) $\begin{bmatrix} 0 \\ -5.1 \end{bmatrix}$ (h) $\begin{bmatrix} -29.8 \\ -119.3 \end{bmatrix}$

3 $\begin{bmatrix} 30.85 \\ 66.16 \end{bmatrix} + \begin{bmatrix} 82.16 \\ 31.54 \end{bmatrix} + \begin{bmatrix} 29.49 \\ -39.13 \end{bmatrix} = \begin{bmatrix} 142.50 \\ 58.57 \end{bmatrix}$

154 km at $22°$ to the x-axis

4 $\begin{bmatrix} 20 \\ 0 \end{bmatrix} + \begin{bmatrix} 11.24 \\ 27.82 \end{bmatrix} + \begin{bmatrix} 8.75 \\ -4.85 \end{bmatrix} = \begin{bmatrix} 39.99 \\ 22.97 \end{bmatrix}$

46 N at 30° to the direction of the 20 N force

5   (a) $\begin{bmatrix} 10 \\ 0 \end{bmatrix} + \begin{bmatrix} 0 \\ -8 \end{bmatrix} + \begin{bmatrix} -2.82 \\ 5.30 \end{bmatrix} = \begin{bmatrix} 7.18 \\ -2.70 \end{bmatrix}$

7.7 N at −21° to the 10 N force

(b) $\begin{bmatrix} -10 \\ 0 \end{bmatrix} + \begin{bmatrix} 0 \\ 12 \end{bmatrix} + \begin{bmatrix} 14.26 \\ 7.26 \end{bmatrix} + \begin{bmatrix} 14.26 \\ -7.26 \end{bmatrix} = \begin{bmatrix} 18.52 \\ 12 \end{bmatrix}$

22 N at 33° to the direction of the dotted line.

6   (a) $\begin{bmatrix} 339.6 \\ -84.7 \end{bmatrix}$ (b) $\begin{bmatrix} 339.6 \\ 84.7 \end{bmatrix}$ (c) $\begin{bmatrix} -370.9 \\ 149.8 \end{bmatrix}$ (d) $\begin{bmatrix} -272.3 \\ -419.3 \end{bmatrix}$

7 $\begin{bmatrix} 513.5 \\ 197.1 \end{bmatrix} + \begin{bmatrix} 12.5 \\ 58.7 \end{bmatrix} = \begin{bmatrix} 526.0 \\ 255.8 \end{bmatrix}$

585 km h^{-1} on a course of 064°

8   (a) $\begin{bmatrix} 240.7 \\ -319.5 \end{bmatrix} + \begin{bmatrix} 0 \\ 80 \end{bmatrix} = \begin{bmatrix} 240.7 \\ -239.5 \end{bmatrix}$

340 km h^{-1} on a course of 135°

(b) $\begin{bmatrix} -472.8 \\ 369.4 \end{bmatrix} + \begin{bmatrix} -21.9 \\ 44.9 \end{bmatrix} = \begin{bmatrix} -494.7 \\ 414.3 \end{bmatrix}$

645 km h^{-1} on a course of 310°

(c) $\begin{bmatrix} -585.1 \\ -545.6 \end{bmatrix} + \begin{bmatrix} -69.5 \\ -8.5 \end{bmatrix} = \begin{bmatrix} -654.6 \\ -554.1 \end{bmatrix}$

858 km h^{-1} on a course of 230°

Vector triangles

1   Angle CBD = 75 − 22 = 53°

CD = 65 sin 53° = 51.9 km   BD = 65 cos 53° = 39.1 km

AD = 90 + 39.1 = 129.1 km   AC = $\sqrt{(51.9^2 + 129.1^2)}$ = 139 km

Angle CAD = $\tan^{-1}\left(\frac{51.9}{129.1}\right)$ = 21.9°

AC = AB + BC = $\begin{bmatrix} 83.4 \\ 33.7 \end{bmatrix} + \begin{bmatrix} 16.8 \\ 62.8 \end{bmatrix} = \begin{bmatrix} 100.2 \\ 96.5 \end{bmatrix}$

i.e. 139 km at 43.9° to the *x*-axis. The answers agree.

2   17.9 N at 23.3° to the 8 N force

3   (a)   29.1 N at 63.5° to the 20 N force

   (b)   44.1 N at 44.5° to the 15 N force

4   351 km h⁻¹ on a course of 040°.

5   Angle ACB = 100°

   BD = 70 sin 80° = 68.9   CD = 70 cos 80° = 12.2

   Angle CAB = $\sin^{-1}\left(\frac{68.9}{400}\right)$ = 9.9°

   AD = 400 cos 9.9° = 394.0   AC = 394.0 – 12.2 = 381.8

   The course to steer is 020° and the speed made good is 382 km h⁻¹.

6   (a)   Course to steer = 084°

      Speed made good = 524 km h⁻¹

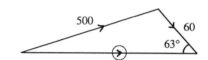

   (b)   Course to steer = 063°

      Speed made good = 504 km h⁻¹

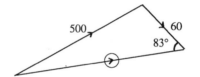

   (c)   Course to steer = 199°

      Speed made good = 287 km h⁻¹

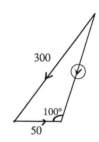

   (d)   Course to steer = 143°

      Speed made good = 403 km h⁻¹

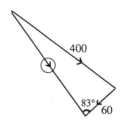

Mean and variance formulas

1

$$\frac{1}{n}\Sigma(x-m)^2 = \frac{1}{n}\Sigma(x^2 - 2mx + m^2)$$

$$= \frac{1}{n}[\Sigma x^2 - \Sigma 2mx + \Sigma m^2]$$

$$= \frac{1}{n}[\Sigma x^2 - 2m\Sigma x + m^2 n]$$

$$= \frac{1}{n}[\Sigma x^2 - 2m \times mn + m^2 n]$$

$$= \frac{1}{n}[\Sigma x^2 - m^2 n]$$

$$= \frac{1}{n}\Sigma x^2 - m^2$$

2

$$\frac{1}{n}\Sigma(x-m)^2 f = \frac{1}{n}[\Sigma x^2 f - \Sigma 2mxf + \Sigma m^2 f]$$

$$= \frac{1}{n}[\Sigma x^2 f - 2m\Sigma xf + m^2 \Sigma f]$$

$$= \frac{1}{n}[\Sigma x^2 f - 2m \times mn + m^2 n]$$

$$= \frac{1}{n}\Sigma x^2 f - m^2$$

3

$$\Sigma(x-\mu)^2 P(x) = \Sigma x^2 P(x) - 2\mu \Sigma x P(x) + \mu^2 \Sigma P(x)$$

$$= \Sigma x^2 P(x) - 2\mu^2 + \mu^2$$

$$= \Sigma x^2 P(x) - \mu^2$$

4

$$m' = \frac{\Sigma(x-k)f}{n} = \frac{\Sigma xf - k\Sigma f}{n} = \frac{\Sigma xf - kn}{n} = \frac{\Sigma xf}{n} - k = m - k$$

Hence $\frac{1}{n}\Sigma(x-k-m')^2 f = \frac{1}{n}\Sigma(x-m)^2 f$

This is easier than basing the proof on the alternative version of the variance formula starting with $\frac{1}{n}\Sigma(x-k)^2 f - m'^2$.

5 $s^2 = \frac{1}{n}\Sigma x^2 - m^2$ gives $\Sigma x^2 = 10(6^2 + 14^2) = 2320$

For the second set, the sum of squares $= 15(4^2 + 19^2) = 5655$

For the combined population, the sum of squares $= 2320 + 5655$
$$= 7975$$

The mean of the combined population is $\frac{10 \times 14 + 15 \times 19}{25} = 17$, which divides the interval from 14 to 19 in the ratio 15 : 10.

The standard deviation of the combined population is $\sqrt{\left(\frac{7975}{25} - 17^2\right)} = 5.48$.

This happens to lie between the individual standard deviations, but this need not be so. Try changing the second mean to 29, leaving the other data unchanged.

Sampling without replacement

1 For the given data, $m = 1.36$, $S = 0.82$.

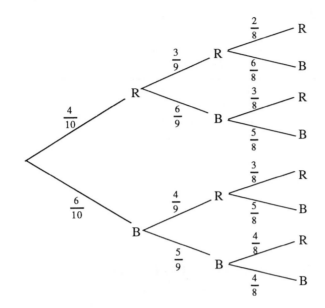

$\mu = 1.2$
$\sigma^2 = 0.56$

Number of reds	Probability	Predicted frequency
0	$\frac{120}{720} = \frac{5}{30}$	$\frac{5}{30} \times 50 \approx 8$
1	$\frac{360}{720} = \frac{15}{30}$	25
2	$\frac{216}{720} = \frac{9}{30}$	15
3	$\frac{24}{720} = \frac{1}{30}$	$\frac{1}{30} \times 50 \approx 2$
	1	50

2

Number of reds	Probability	Predicted frequency
0	$\frac{210}{720}$	15
1	$\frac{378}{720}$	26
2	$\frac{126}{720}$	9
3	$\frac{6}{720}$	0
	1	50

$\mu = 0.9$
$\sigma^2 = 0.49$

3   The smallest possible score is 1 and the largest is 9. Since small numbers are more likely than large ones (as will become clear), the mean will be nearer 1, between 3 and 4, for example

$$P(4) \ = \ \frac{8}{10} \times \frac{7}{9} \times \frac{6}{8} \times \frac{2}{7} \ = \ \frac{6}{45}$$

Score	1	2	3	4	5	6	7	8	9
Probability	$\frac{9}{45}$	$\frac{8}{45}$	$\frac{7}{45}$	$\frac{6}{45}$	$\frac{5}{45}$	$\frac{4}{45}$	$\frac{3}{45}$	$\frac{2}{45}$	$\frac{1}{45}$
Predicted frequency	18	16	14	12	10	8	6	4	2

Predicted mean $= \mu = 3\frac{2}{3}$

4   This time there is no theoretical maximum score.

Score	1	2	3	4	5	6	...
Probability	$\frac{1}{5}$	$\left(\frac{4}{5}\right)\left(\frac{1}{5}\right)$	$\left(\frac{4}{5}\right)^2\left(\frac{1}{5}\right)$	$\left(\frac{4}{5}\right)^3\left(\frac{1}{5}\right)$	$\left(\frac{4}{5}\right)^4\left(\frac{1}{5}\right)$	$\left(\frac{4}{5}\right)^5\left(\frac{1}{5}\right)$	...
Predicted frequency	18	14.4	11.5	9.2	7.4	5.9	...

The theoretical mean (the calculation of which involves a simple program or summing an infinite series) is now 5.

5   For each score, the predicted frequency will lie between the corresponding ones for questions 3 and 4. In (a), they will be closer to those of question 3, while in (b), the results will be similar to those of question 4.

For example, in (b) $P(4) \ = \ \frac{80}{100} \times \frac{79}{99} \times \frac{78}{98} \times \frac{20}{97} \ \approx \ \frac{4}{5} \times \frac{4}{5} \times \frac{4}{5} \times \frac{1}{5}$

6

Number of reds	Probability	Predicted frequency
0	$\left(\frac{6}{10}\right)^3$	10.8
1	$3\left(\frac{6}{10}\right)^2\left(\frac{4}{10}\right)$	21.6
2	$3\left(\frac{6}{10}\right)\left(\frac{4}{10}\right)^2$	14.4
3	$\left(\frac{4}{10}\right)^3$	3.2
	1	50

$\mu = 1.2, \quad \sigma^2 = 0.72$

7   Sampling with replacement means that a name may be picked for a sample more than once and the opinion expressed should then be counted accordingly. As in question 5(b), when the 'parent population' is large enough, it does not matter in practice whether samples are taken with or without replacement.

8   The probability that 4 throws are needed to obtain an even number is $\frac{1}{16}$.

On average, $\sum x\,P(x) = 1 \times \frac{1}{2} + 2 \times \frac{1}{4} + 3 \times \frac{1}{8} + \dots$

$$= 2$$

(A calculator can easily be programmed to add, for example, 20 terms of this series.)

Throwing until a six appears, $P(4) = \left(\frac{5}{6}\right)^3 \left(\frac{1}{6}\right)$

Now $\mu = \sum x\,P(x) = 6$

The series for μ converges less rapidly now, and more terms must be taken to obtain a convincing answer.

9   The St Petersburg paradox is based upon a gambling game reputed to have been played by the aristocrats of St Petersburg. The game can be played as follows.

For the payment of an initial stake, a player has the right to toss a coin repeatedly until a head appears. If it comes down head first time, the player wins 1p; the sequence TH gains 2p, TTH is worth 4p, TTTH 8p etc. If the first head occurs after n tails, the player wins 2^n p.

The surprising result which intrigued the gamblers of St Petersburg was that no original stake could be large enough to make the game fair, assuming unlimited resources of time and money. You might like to try check this result by simulating the game on a computer or programmable calculator.

On average, a player wins

$$\sum x\,P(x) = 1 \times \frac{1}{2} + 2 \times \frac{1}{4} + 4 \times \frac{1}{8} + \dots$$
$$= \frac{1}{2} + \frac{1}{2} + \frac{1}{2} + \dots$$

The player can therefore expect to win, on average, an infinite amount.

Sine and cosine rules

1 (a) Just over $10.3 - 7.6 = 2.7$ cm; the cosine rule gives 3.32 cm.

(b) 12.1 cm; approximately $\sqrt{(10^2 + 7^2)}$.

(c) 17.5 cm; a little less than $7.6 + 10.3 = 17.9$ cm.

2 (a) 38.3°   (b) 121.9°

3 (a) (i) −1.04

(ii) α cannot be found because the triangle is impossible. This can be spotted immediately, since $325 + 459 < 791$.

(b) $\cos \beta = 1.006$ according to the cosine rule. This is again an impossible value.

4 (a) 10.9 cm   (b) 8.43 cm   (c) 8.43 cm

In (a), you should expect x to be a little more than 9.1 cm. The other answers are equal because $\sin 74° = \sin 106°$ and if the two triangles are combined as shown, an isoceles triangle is obtained on the left.

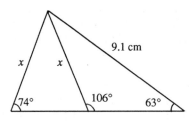

5 (a) 43.4°   (b) 74.9° or 105.1°   (c) Impossible data

6 (a) $B = 68.9°$ or $111.1°$, $C = 180° - (68.9° + 49°) = 62.1°$ or $180° - (111.1° + 49°) = 19.9°$, $c = 6.44$ cm or 2.48 cm

(b) $5.5^2 = 6.8^2 + c^2 - 2 \times 6.8 \times c \times \cos 49°$
Therefore $c^2 - 8.922c + 15.99 = 0$ with solutions 6.44 and 2.48.
Then $B = 68.9°$ or $111.1°$ and $C = 62.1°$ or $19.9°$.

7

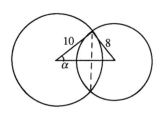

$$\cos \alpha = \frac{100 + 169 - 64}{260}$$

$$\alpha = 38.0°$$

Radius of circle $= 10 \sin \alpha$

$$= 6.15 \text{ cm}$$

8

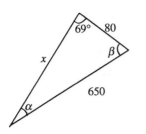

$\alpha = 6.6°, \quad \beta = 104.4°$

$x = 674$

The course to steer is 035°.
The speed is 674 km h^{-1}.

9 (a)

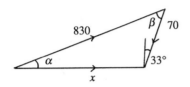

$\alpha = 4.1°, \quad \beta = 52.9°$

$x = 790$

The course to steer is 086°.
The speed is 790 km h^{-1}.

(b)

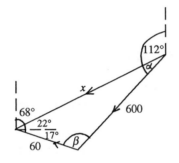

$\alpha = 3.6°, \quad \beta = 137.4°$

$x = 645$

The course to steer is 244°.
The speed is 645 km h^{-1}.

Trigonometric identities

1 (a) The formula $\frac{1}{2}ab \sin C$ takes the form $\frac{1}{2}pq \sin (A + B)$.

(b) $LN = p \sin A$, $ON = q \cos B$, area of triangle $OLN = \frac{1}{2} pq \sin A \cos B$

(c) Similarly, $MN = q \sin B$, $ON = p \cos A$, area of triangle $OMN = \frac{1}{2}pq \cos A \sin B$

(d) Triangle OLM = triangle OLN + triangle OMN
Therefore $\sin (A + B) = \sin A \cos B + \cos A \sin B$.

2 (a) Angle $GFJ = 2A$, so $GJ = \sin 2A$, $FJ = \cos 2A$.

(b) $OG = 2 \cos A$, $GJ = 2 \sin A \cos A$, $OJ = 2 \cos^2 A$, $FJ = 2 \cos^2 A - 1$
Hence $\sin 2A = 2 \sin A \cos A$, $\cos 2A = 2 \cos^2 A - 1$.

3 $\frac{dy}{dx} = \cos x \cos \alpha - \sin x \sin \alpha \ (= \cos (x + \alpha)$ as expected).

$\frac{d^2y}{dx^2} = -\sin x \cos \alpha - \cos x \sin \alpha \ (= -\sin (x + \alpha))$.

4 $\dfrac{d}{dx} (\sin x \cos x) = \cos^2 x - \sin^2 x$ $(= \cos 2x$, the derivative of $\frac{1}{2} \sin 2x)$

     $\dfrac{d}{dx} (\sin^2 x) = 2 \sin x \cos x$ $(= \sin 2x$, the derivative of $\frac{1}{2}(1 - \cos 2x))$

     $\dfrac{d}{dx} (\cos^2 x) = -2 \sin x \cos x$ $(= - \sin 2x$, the derivative of $\frac{1}{2}(1 + \cos 2x))$

Since $\sin^2 x + \cos^2 x = 1$ for all x, the derivatives of $\sin^2 x$ and $\cos^2 x$ should add to zero.

5

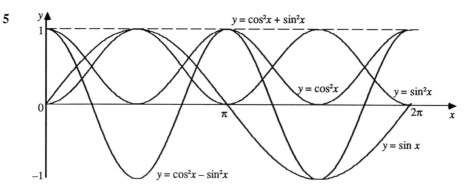

The graphs are periodic and repeat to the left of 0 and to the right of 2π.

It is tempting to show the graphs of $y = \sin^2 x$ and $y = \cos^2 x$ as a series of hoops but they are smoothly rounded near their lowest points. The relation $\sin^2 x + \cos^2 x = 1$ reinforces this message, as does $\sin^2 x = \frac{1}{2} (1 - \cos 2x)$ (see question 6).

The graph of $\cos^2 x - \sin^2 x = \cos 2x$ is a cosine graph with period π and amplitude 1.

6

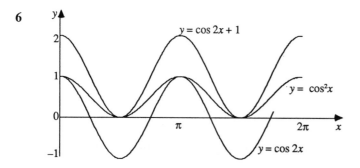

These graphs illustrate the relation:

$$\cos^2 x = \frac{1}{2}(\cos 2x + 1)$$

7   (a)   This is a sine wave with period π because $2 \sin x \cos x = \sin 2x$.

     (b)   This is a standard sine wave translated 0.5 to the right because
         $\sin x \cos 0.5 - \cos x \sin 0.5 = \sin (x - 0.5)$.

     (c)   This is a standard cosine wave translated 0.5 to the right because
         $\cos x \cos 0.5 - \sin x \sin 0.5 = \cos (x - 0.5)$

8   (a) $\displaystyle\int_0^{\pi/2} \frac{1}{2} \sin 2x \, dx = \left[-\frac{1}{4} \cos 2x \right]_0^{\pi/2} = \frac{1}{4} + \frac{1}{4} = \frac{1}{2}$

     (b) $\displaystyle\int_0^{\pi} \frac{1}{2} (1 + \cos 2x) \, dx = \left[\frac{1}{2} x + \frac{1}{4} \sin 2x \right]_0^{\pi} = \frac{1}{2} \pi$

(c) $\displaystyle\int_0^{\pi/4} \frac{1}{2}(1 - \cos 2x)\,dx = \left[\frac{1}{2}x - \frac{1}{4}\sin 2x\right]_0^{\pi/4} = \frac{1}{8}\pi - \frac{1}{4}$

9 $2 \sin 2x = \cos x$ means $4 \sin x \cos x = \cos x$

$\cos x = 0$ or $\sin x = \frac{1}{4}$

x is 0.253, 1.57, 2.89 or 4.71

10 (a) $4 \cos^2 x - 2 = 3 \cos x - 2 \Rightarrow \cos x = 0$ or $\frac{3}{4}$

x is 0.723, 1.57, 4.71 or 5.56

(b) $1 - 2 \sin^2 x = 3 \sin x \Rightarrow 2 \sin^2 x + 3 \sin x - 1 = 0 \Rightarrow \sin x = \frac{-3 \pm \sqrt{17}}{4}$

Then $x = 0.285$ or 2.86 because $\sin x$ cannot equal $\frac{-3 - \sqrt{17}}{4}$.

11 $\cos(A + B) + \cos(A - B) = \cos A \cos B - \sin A \sin B + \cos A \cos B + \sin A \sin B$
$$= 2 \cos A \cos B$$

$\displaystyle\int_0^{\pi/4} \cos 2x \cos x \, dx = \int_0^{\pi/4} \frac{1}{2}(\cos 3x + \cos x)\,dx$

$$= \left[\frac{1}{6}\sin 3x + \frac{1}{2}\sin x\right]_0^{\pi/4} = \frac{1}{3}\sqrt{2} = 0.471$$

$\displaystyle\int_0^{\pi/2} \cos 2x \cos x \, dx = \frac{1}{3}$

The graph of $y = \cos 2x \cos x$ is below the x-axis between $x = \frac{1}{4}\pi$ and $x = \frac{1}{2}\pi$, which is why the second integral gives a smaller answer than the first.

12 $\frac{dy}{dx} = -2 \sin 2x \cos x - \cos 2x \sin x$

$= -4 \sin x \cos^2 x - \sin x \,(\cos^2 x - \sin^2 x)$

$= \sin x \,(-5 \cos^2 x + \sin^2 x)$

$= 0$ when $\sin x = 0$ or $\tan^2 x = 5$ (equivalent to $\cos^2 x = \frac{1}{6}$ or $\sin^2 x = \frac{5}{6}$)

x is 0, 1.15, 1.99, π, 4.29, 5.13 or 2π.

Further trigonometry

1 (a) $\alpha = 51.3°$, $\beta = 102.6°$, $\gamma = 26.0°$; $\beta = 2\alpha$

(b) When $x = 0.2$, the longest side is greater than the sum of the other two sides and the triangle cannot be drawn.

(c) $x + \sqrt{x} > 1 - x \Rightarrow x > (1 - 2x)^2$, i.e. $4x^2 - 5x + 1 < 0$ or $0.25 < x < 1$.
Also, $x + (1 - x) > \sqrt{x} \Rightarrow x < 1$, and $\sqrt{x} + (1 - x) > x \Rightarrow x > (2x - 1)^2$. So $0.25 < x < 1$.

(d) $\cos \alpha = \dfrac{1-2x+x^2+x-x^2}{2(1-x)\sqrt{x}} = \dfrac{1-x}{2(1-x)\sqrt{x}} = \dfrac{1}{2\sqrt{x}}$

$\cos \beta = \dfrac{1-2x+x^2+x^2-x}{2x(1-x)} = \dfrac{(1-x)(1-2x)}{2x(1-x)} = \dfrac{1}{2x} - 1$

(e) $2\cos^2 \alpha - 1 = 2\left(\dfrac{1}{4x}\right) - 1 = \cos \beta$

(f) $\dfrac{\sqrt{x}}{\sin \beta} = \dfrac{x}{\sin \alpha} \Rightarrow \sin \beta = \dfrac{\sin \alpha}{\sqrt{x}} = 2 \sin \alpha \cos \alpha$

(g) The double angle formulas show that $\beta = 2\alpha$ for any acceptable value of x.

2 (a) The length of a side is $2 \sin \theta$, with θ starting as $30°$ and being halved repeatedly.

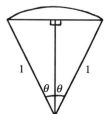

(b) $\sin 2\theta = 2 \sin \theta \cos \theta = 2 \sin \theta \sqrt{(1 - \sin^2\theta)}$
So $2 \sin 2\theta = 2 \sin \theta \sqrt{(4 - 4 \sin^2\theta)}$
Hence $X^2 = x^2 (4 - x^2)$.

(c) $x^4 - 4x^2 = - X^2$, so $x^4 - 4x^2 + 4 = 4 - X^2$
$x^2 - 2 = - \sqrt{(4 - X^2)}$, the negative sign being required because $x^2 < 2$.
$x = \sqrt{(2 - \sqrt{(4 - X^2)})}$

(d) $2 \sin 30° = 1$ and the inductive relation follows from (c).

(e) The circumference of the circle is 2π, so half the perimeter of the regular hexagon, dodecahedron etc. is required. This gives the stated sequence.

(f) Increasing the number of sides of the polygon works well at first and the perimeter of a 3072–sided regular polygon suggests $\pi \approx 3.141593$. Thereafter, rounding errors seriously erode the accuracy of the approximations to π.

(g) This sequence is based upon starting with a square and proceeding to use 8, 16, 32, ... sided regular polygons. This is also successful at first but runs into the same problems.

3 (a) This requires repeated use of the formula $\sin 2A = 2 \sin A \cos A$.

(b) $\cos 2A = 2 \cos^2 A - 1$ and so $2 \cos 2A = (2 \cos A)^2 - 2$. Then $U = u^2 - 2$ and $u = \sqrt{(U + 2)}$.

(c) $u_0 = \sqrt{3} = 2 \cos 30°$, $u_1 = \sqrt{(\sqrt{3} + 2)} = 2 \cos 15°$. The given sequence is $u_2 = 2 \cos 7.5°$, $u_3 = 2 \cos 3.75°$, ...

Since $2 \sin 30° = 1$, $2 \sin 15° = \dfrac{1}{u_1}$, $2 \sin 7.5° = \dfrac{1}{u_1 u_2}$, $2 \sin 3.75° = \dfrac{1}{u_1 u_2 u_3}$ and the semi-perimeters of regular 6, 12, 24, 48, ... sided polygons inscribed in a circle of radius 1 are given by $3, \dfrac{6}{u_1}, \dfrac{12}{u_1 u_2}, \dfrac{24}{u_1 u_2 u_3}, ...$

(d) To move on from one approximation to the next, you need to double and divide by the new term of the u-sequence, as in the programs. The calculated sequence converges to π. This time, rounding errors are not significant.

(e) The initial values should be 0 and 2.

There are many other methods for calculating π through simple programs. You might like to investigate them for a project.

Air resistance

1 (a) The graph is a straight line with gradient -10.

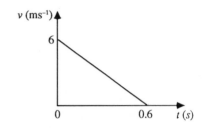

(b) The time for the speed to reduce to zero is 0.6 seconds and the height risen (which is represented by the area under the graph) is 1.8 metres.

2 (a) $\frac{dv}{dt}$ is the acceleration of the stone. The negative sign is required in the differential equation because v is taken to be in the upwards direction and gravity acts downwards. Integrating $\frac{dv}{dt} = -10$ gives $v = -10t + c$, where c ms^{-1} is the velocity when $t = 0$, i.e. $c = 6$.

(b) In $\frac{dv}{dt} = -10 - 0.4v$, it is assumed that there is an air resistance force equal to $0.4v$ times the mass of the stone. The negative sign indicates that this force acts downwards.

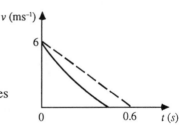

The initial acceleration is $-10 - 2.4 = -12.4$ ms^{-2} and as v approaches zero, the acceleration approaches -10 ms^{-2}. The solution curve starts more steeply than that in question 1 and ends parallel with it.

3

t	v	$\frac{dv}{dt} = -10 - 0.4v$	dt	dv
0	6	-12.4	0.1	-1.24
0.1	4.76	-11.9	0.1	-1.19
0.2	3.57	-11.4	0.1	-1.14
0.3	2.43	-11.0	0.1	-1.10
0.4	1.33	-10.5	0.1	-1.05
0.5	0.28			

With a deceleration of about 10 ms^{-2}, the final 0.28 ms^{-1} will be lost in about 0.03 seconds, giving a total time for the upward flight of 0.53 seconds.

The numerical method is inherently inaccurate so it is pointless to retain more decimal places in the calculation.

4 (a) $\dfrac{dv}{dt} = -0.4\,(25 + v) \Rightarrow \dfrac{dt}{dv} = -\dfrac{1}{0.4} \times \dfrac{1}{25 + v}$

$$= -2.5 \times \dfrac{1}{25 + v}$$

   (b) $t = -2.5 \ln (25 + v) + A$ where $0 = -2.5 \ln (25 + 6) + A \Rightarrow A = 2.5 \ln 31 \approx 8.585.$

When $v = 0$, $t = -2.5 \ln 25 + 2.5 \ln 31 = 0.538$ (to 3 s.f.)

This answer is greater than the answer in question 3 because the numerical method uses the gradient at the beginning of each interval instead of the average gradient for the interval. Consequently it reduces the speed slightly too rapidly. The time is obviously greater in question 1 because there is no air resistance.

5 (a) $t = -2.5 \ln (25 + v) + 2.5 \ln 31 \Rightarrow -0.4t = \ln (25 + v) - \ln 31 = \ln\left(\dfrac{25 + v}{31}\right)$

Hence $\dfrac{25 + v}{31} = e^{-0.4t}$ and $v = 31\,e^{-0.4t} - 25.$

   (b) Integrating gives $y = -\dfrac{31}{0.4}\,e^{-0.4t} - 25t + B$, where $B = \dfrac{31}{0.4}$ if the height y is taken as 0 when $t = 0$.

Putting $t = 0.538$ now gives $y = 1.55$ metres. This is a little smaller than the height calculated in question 1, as one would expect.

6 $\dfrac{dt}{dv} = -2 \times \dfrac{1}{20 + v} \Rightarrow t = -2 \ln (20 + v) + 2 \ln 26.$ $t = 0.525$ when $v = 0$.

$v = 26\,e^{-0.5t} - 20$ gives $y = -52\,e^{-0.5t} - 20t + B$, when $B = 52$. The total height is now 1.51 m.

7

t	v	$\dfrac{dv}{dt} = 10 - 0.4v$	dt	dv
0	0	10	0.1	1
0.1	1	9.6	0.1	0.96
0.2	1.96	9.2	0.1	0.92
0.3	2.88	8.8	0.1	0.88
0.4	3.76	8.5	0.1	0.85
0.5	4.61	8.2	0.1	0.82
0.6	5.43	7.8	0.1	0.78
0.7	6.21			

The overall change in velocity is, of course, less here than in question 3.

8 $\dfrac{dt}{dv} = \dfrac{1}{0.4} \times \dfrac{1}{25 - v} \Rightarrow t = -2.5 \ln (25 - v) + A$, and $A = 2.5 \ln 25$ if $v = 0$ when $t = 0$.

Then $v = 6$ when $t = 0.686$, a result consistent with the answers to question 7.

9 $v = 25\,(1 - e^{-0.4t}) = 4.53$ when $t = 0.5$. As expected, this is marginally less than the approximate answer found in question 7.

$y = 25t + 62.5\,e^{-0.4t} - 62.5$ (if $y = 0$ when $t = 0$)
$y = 2.15$ when $t = 0.686$

10 As v approaches 25, $\frac{dv}{dt}$ approaches 0. The solution curve is as shown, with $v = 25$ as an asymptote.

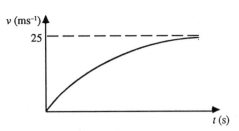

Given $\frac{dv}{dt} = 10 - 0.5v = 0.5\,(20 - v)$, the terminal velocity is 20 ms^{-1}. The increased air resistance means a lower terminal velocity.

Tan and sec

1 $\tan \frac{\pi}{4} = 1$, $\sec \frac{\pi}{4} = \sqrt{2}$, $\tan \frac{\pi}{6} = \frac{1}{\sqrt{3}}$, $\tan \frac{\pi}{3} = \sqrt{3}$, $\sec \frac{\pi}{3} = 2$

2 $1 + \tan^2 x = 1 + \frac{\sin^2 x}{\cos^2 x} = \frac{\cos^2 x + \sin^2 x}{\cos^2 x} = \frac{1}{\cos^2 x} = \sec^2 x$

3 $y = \frac{\sin x}{\cos x} \Rightarrow \frac{dy}{dx} = \frac{\cos^2 x + \sin^2 x}{\cos^2 x} = \sec^2 x$

$y = \frac{1}{\cos x} \Rightarrow \frac{dy}{dx} = \frac{\sin x}{\cos^2 x} = \sec x \tan x$

4 $y = \ln (\sec x) \Rightarrow \frac{dy}{dx} = \frac{\sec x \tan x}{\sec x} = \tan x$

$y = \ln (\sec x + \tan x) \Rightarrow \frac{dy}{dx} = \frac{\sec x \tan x + \sec^2 x}{\sec x + \tan x} = \sec x$

5

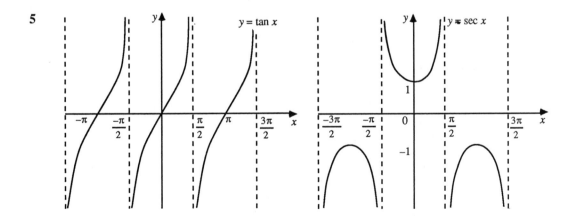

6 (a) $\sec^2 \frac{\pi}{4} = 2$ (b) $\sec (-\frac{\pi}{4}) \tan (-\frac{\pi}{4}) = -1.41$

(c) 2.03 (d) $2 \tan 1.3 \sec^2 1.3 = 101$ (e) 101

7 (a) $\tan \frac{\pi}{4} = 1$

(b) $\left[\ln (\sec x + \tan x) \right]_0^{\pi/4} = 0.881$

(c) 0   (d) 0.268   (e) 2.69

8 (a) The graph is a reflection in $y = x$ of just one branch of the graph of $y = \tan x$.

(b) $\frac{dx}{dy} = \sec^2 y = 1 + \tan^2 y$
$= 1 + x^2$

Hence $\frac{dy}{dx} = \frac{1}{1 + x^2}$

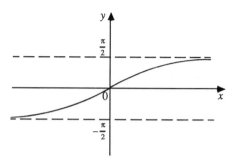

9 $x = a \tan u$ gives $\frac{dx}{du} = a \sec^2 u$ so in the integral dx must be replaced by $a \sec^2 u \, du$.

$$\int \frac{1}{a^2 + x^2} \, dx = \int \frac{a \sec^2 u}{a^2 + a^2 \tan^2 u} \, du = \int \frac{a \sec^2 u}{a^2 \sec^2 u} \, du = \int \frac{1}{a} \, du = \frac{1}{a} \tan^{-1} \frac{x}{a} + c$$

10 (a) $\frac{1}{4}\left(1 + \frac{1}{1 + 1/4}\right) + \frac{1}{4}\left(\frac{1}{1 + 1/4} + \frac{1}{1 + 1}\right) = 0.775$

(b) $\frac{1}{2}\left(\frac{1}{1 + 1/16}\right) + \frac{1}{2}\left(\frac{1}{1 + 9/16}\right) = 0.791$

The correct area is $\int_0^1 \frac{1}{1 + x^2} \, dx = \tan^{-1} 1 = \frac{\pi}{4} \approx 0.785$

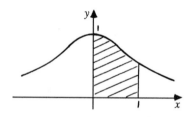

11 (a)

t	v	$\frac{dv}{dt}$	dt	dv
0	8	− 16.4	0.1	− 1.64
0.1	6.36	− 14.0	0.1	− 1.40
0.2	4.96	− 12.5	0.1	− 1.25
0.3	3.71	− 11.4	0.1	− 1.14
0.4	2.57	− 10.7	0.1	− 1.07
0.5	1.50	− 10.2	0.1	− 1.02
0.6	0.48			

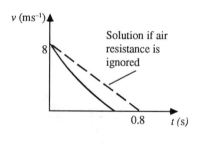

The table suggests the time to the highest point is about 0.65 seconds.

(b) $t = -\frac{10}{10} \tan^{-1}\left(\frac{v}{10}\right) + A$ where $A = \tan^{-1} 0.8$ since $v = 8$ initially. Consequently,

when $v = 0$, $t = \tan^{-1} 0.8 = 0.675$.

(c) $v = -10 \tan (t - A)$
$y = -10 \ln \sec (t - A) + B$ where $B = 10 \ln \sec (-A)$
Then when $t = 0.675$, $y = 10 \ln \sec (-A) = 2.47$.

Calculus techniques

1 (a) $15(3x+4)^4$ (b) $\frac{3}{2}(3x+4)^{-\frac{1}{2}}$ (c) $15x^2(x^3+4)^4$

(d) $\frac{5}{3}x^{-\frac{2}{3}}(x^{\frac{1}{3}}+4)^4$ (e) $3e^{3x}$ (f) $\frac{3}{3x+4}$

(g) $12\cos(4x+5)$ (h) $-3x^{-\frac{1}{2}}\sin(6\sqrt{x}+7)$ (i) $\frac{1}{2}\sec^2x\,(\tan x)^{-\frac{1}{2}}$

(j) $\frac{1}{2}x^{-\frac{1}{2}}\sec^2(\sqrt{x})$ (k) $\frac{2}{3}x(x^2-4)^{-\frac{2}{3}}$ (l) $\frac{d}{dx}(x^{\frac{3}{2}}+8x)=\frac{3}{2}x^{\frac{1}{2}}+8$

(m) $2xe^{3x}+3x^2e^{3x}+16x$

(n) $e^{x\ln x}\times\frac{d}{dx}(x\ln x)=e^{x\ln x}(\ln x+1)$. Note that $e^{x\ln x}=x^x$

(o) $\frac{1}{1+x^2/36}\times\frac{1}{6}=\frac{6}{36+x^2}$ (p) $\frac{1}{\sqrt{(1-x^2/100)}}\times\frac{1}{10}=\frac{1}{\sqrt{(100-x^2)}}$

Constants of integration are omitted in the answers to the next three questions.

2 (a) $\frac{1}{16}(4x-1)^4$ (b) $\frac{1}{4}e^{4x-1}$ (c) $\frac{9}{4}\sin(4x-1)$

(d) $\int(4x^2-x)\,dx=\frac{4}{3}x^3-\frac{1}{2}x^2$ (e) $\frac{8}{5}x^{\frac{5}{2}}-\frac{2}{3}x^{\frac{3}{2}}$

(f) $\frac{1}{6}(4x-1)^{\frac{3}{2}}$ (g) $\frac{1}{12}(4x^2-1)^{\frac{3}{2}}$

(h) $\int(16x^4-8x^2+1)\,dx=\frac{16}{5}x^5-\frac{8}{3}x^3+x$ (no other methods are suitable)

(i) $\frac{1}{4}\ln|4x-1|$ (j) $\frac{1}{2}(4x-1)^{\frac{1}{2}}$ (k) $\frac{1}{2}\ln(3+x^2)$

(l) $(3+x^2)^{\frac{1}{2}}$ (m) $\frac{6}{\sqrt{3}}\tan^{-1}\left(\frac{x}{\sqrt{3}}\right)$ (see question 1 (o))

(n) $6\sin^{-1}\left(\frac{x}{\sqrt{3}}\right)$ (see question 1 (p))   (o) $-e^{-\frac{1}{2}x^2}$

3 (a) $x=\frac{u+2}{3}$ so replace dx by $\frac{1}{3}du$

$I=\frac{1}{9}\int(u^{\frac{3}{2}}+2u^{\frac{1}{2}})\,du=\frac{2}{45}(3x-2)^{\frac{5}{2}}+\frac{4}{27}(3x-2)^{\frac{3}{2}}$

(b) Replace dx by $2(u-2)\,du$

$I=20\int(1-\frac{2}{u})\,du=20(\sqrt{x}+2)-40\ln(\sqrt{x}+2)$

(c) $I=\tan^{-1}u=\tan^{-1}\left(\frac{2}{3}x\right)$ (d) Let $u=x+2$. $I=\ln|x+2|+\frac{3}{x+2}$

(e) Let $u=e^x+3$. $I=-\frac{1}{e^x+3}$ (f) $\ln(e^x+3)+\frac{3}{e^x+3}$

63

(g)　Replace dx by $2 \sec^2 u\, du$

$$I = \int \sec u\, du = \ln |\sec u + \tan u| = \ln \left(\tfrac{1}{2}\sqrt{(4+x^2)} + \tfrac{1}{2}x\right)$$

$$= \ln (\sqrt{(4+x^2)} + x) - \ln 2$$

The full answer is $\ln(\sqrt{(4+x^2)} + x) + c$, for any constant c; the $\ln 2$ may be included or omitted.

(h)　$I = \dfrac{1}{2}\displaystyle\int \sec u\, du = \dfrac{1}{2}\ln|\sec u + \tan u|$

$$= \tfrac{1}{2}\ln\left|\frac{1+\sin u}{\cos u}\right| = \tfrac{1}{2}\ln\left|\frac{1+x/2}{\sqrt{(1-x^2/4)}}\right|$$

$$= \tfrac{1}{2}\ln\sqrt{\left(\frac{1+x/2}{1-x/2}\right)} = \tfrac{1}{4}\ln\left|\frac{2+x}{2-x}\right|$$

Note that the substitution is only legitimate if values of x are limited to $-2 < x < 2$. It is appropriate (and easier) to use partial fractions here.

4　(a)　$\dfrac{2}{9}x(3x-2)^{\frac{3}{2}} - \dfrac{4}{135}(3x-2)^{\frac{5}{2}}$　　　　(b)　$-(x-1)(x+2)^{-1} + \ln|x+2|$

(c)　$\dfrac{1}{5}x^2 e^{5x} - \dfrac{2}{25}x e^{5x} + \dfrac{2}{125}e^{5x}$, using the formula twice.

(d)　$-\dfrac{1}{3}x\cos 3x + \dfrac{1}{9}\sin 3x$　　　　(e)　$x\tan x - \ln|\sec x| = x\tan x + \ln|\cos x|$

(f)　$I = \dfrac{1}{2}\displaystyle\int \left((x+1) - (x+1)\cos 2x\right) dx$

$$= \tfrac{1}{4}x^2 + \tfrac{1}{2}x - \tfrac{1}{4}(x+1)\sin 2x - \tfrac{1}{8}\cos 2x$$

5　(i)　$\dfrac{2}{45}(3x-2)^{\frac{5}{2}} + \dfrac{4}{27}(3x-2)^{\frac{3}{2}}$

$$= \tfrac{1}{135}(3x-2)^{\frac{3}{2}}\left(6(3x-2)+20\right) = \tfrac{1}{135}(3x-2)^{\frac{3}{2}}(18x+8)$$

$$\tfrac{2}{9}x(3x-2)^{\frac{3}{2}} - \tfrac{4}{135}(3x-2)^{\frac{5}{2}} = \tfrac{1}{135}(3x-2)^{\frac{3}{2}}\left(30x - 4(3x-2)\right)$$

$$= \tfrac{1}{135}(3x-2)^{\frac{3}{2}}(18x+8)$$

(ii)　$-(x-1)(x+2)^{-1} + \ln|x+2| = -\dfrac{(x+2)-3}{x+2} + \ln|x+2| = -1 + \dfrac{3}{x+2} + \ln|x+2|$

This differs from the answer to question 3(d) only by a constant.

(iii)　If $I = 20(\sqrt{x}+2) - 40\ln|\sqrt{x}+2|$, then

$$\frac{dI}{dx} = 10x^{-\frac{1}{2}} - \frac{20x^{-\frac{1}{2}}}{\sqrt{x}+2} = \frac{10 + 20x^{-\frac{1}{2}} - 20x^{-\frac{1}{2}}}{\sqrt{x}+2} = \frac{10}{\sqrt{x}+2}$$

$$I = \ln (\sqrt{(4 + x^2)} + x) \Rightarrow \frac{dI}{dx} = \left(\frac{x}{\sqrt{(4 + x^2)}} + 1\right) \div \left(\sqrt{(4 + x^2)} + x\right)$$

$$= \frac{x + \sqrt{(4 + x^2)}}{\sqrt{(4 + x^2)}} \div \left(\sqrt{4 + x^2} + x\right)$$

$$= \frac{1}{\sqrt{(4 + x^2)}}$$

$$I = \frac{1}{4} \ln\left| \frac{2 + x}{2 - x} \right| = \frac{1}{4} \left(\ln| 2 + x | - \ln| 2 - x | \right)$$

$$\Rightarrow \frac{dI}{dx} = \frac{1}{4}\left(\frac{1}{2 + x} + \frac{1}{2 - x}\right) = \frac{1}{4}\left(\frac{2 - x + 2 + x}{(2 + x)(2 - x)}\right) = \frac{1}{4 - x^2}$$

The method of partial fractions applied to the original integral reverses the above steps.

You can see that integrals can quite often be tackled successfully by more than one method.

6     $\int \ln x \, dx = \int u\, e^u \, du = u\, e^u - e^u$ (integrating by parts)

         $= x \ln x - x$

7   (a) $V_1 = \pi \int_0^9 x \, dx = 40\frac{1}{2}\pi ; \quad V_2 = \pi \int_0^3 y^4 \, dy = 48\frac{3}{5}\pi$

    (b) $V_1 = \pi \int_1^4 (x + 4\sqrt{x} + 4) \, dx = 38\frac{1}{6}\pi$

         $V_2 = \pi \int_3^4 (y - 2)^4 \, dy = 6\frac{1}{5}\pi$

    (c) $V_1 = 375\pi, \; V_2 = 125\pi$

    (d) $V_1 = 60\frac{2}{7}\pi, \; V_2 = \pi \int_3^{11} (y - 3)^{\frac{2}{3}} \, dy = 19\frac{1}{5}\pi$

    (e) $V_1 = \frac{1}{3}\pi r h^2, \; V_2 = \frac{1}{3}\pi r^2 h$ (a cone with radius r and height h)

    (f) $V_1 = V_2 = \frac{2}{3}\pi r^3$ (hemispheres)

    (g) $V_1 = V_2 = 1\frac{1}{2}\pi$

    (h) $V_1 = \pi \ln 4, \; V_2 = \pi \int_{1/2}^1 y^{-4} \, dy = 2\frac{1}{3}\pi$

    (i) $V_1 = \pi \int_0^1 e^{2x} \, dx = \frac{1}{2}\pi (e^2 - 1)$

         $V_2 = \pi \int_1^e (\ln y)^2 \, dy = \pi \int_0^1 u^2 e^u \, du$, putting $u = \ln y$

         $= \left[\pi (u^2 e^u - 2u\, e^u + 2\, e^u)\right]_0^1$, integrating by parts

         $= \pi (e - 2)$

(j) $V_1 = \pi \int_0^{\pi/2} \cos^2 x \, dx = \pi \int_0^{\pi/2} \frac{1}{2}(1 + \cos 2x) \, dx = \frac{1}{4}\pi^2$

$V_2 = \pi \int_0^1 (\cos^{-1} y)^2 \, dy = \pi \int_{\pi/2}^0 -u^2 \sin u \, du, \text{ where } u = \cos^{-1} y$

$= \pi \left[u^2 \cos u - 2u \sin u - 2 \cos u \right]_{\pi/2}^0, \text{ integrating by parts twice}$

$= \pi (\pi - 2)$

(k) $V_1 = \pi \int_0^1 \frac{x^2}{(x+1)^2} \, dx = \pi \int_1^2 \frac{(u-1)^2}{u^2} \, du \text{ where } u = x + 1$

$= \pi \int_1^2 \left(1 - \frac{2}{u} + \frac{1}{u^2} \right) du = \left(1\frac{1}{2} - 2 \ln 2 \right)\pi$

$V_2 = \pi \int_0^{1/2} \frac{y^2}{(1-y)^2} \, dy = -\pi \int_1^{1/2} \frac{1 - 2u + u^2}{u^2} \, du, \text{ where } u = 1 - y$

$= \left(1\frac{1}{2} - 2 \ln 2 \right)\pi = V_1$

8 (a) $V_1 = \pi \int_0^1 e^{2x^2} \, dx \approx 2.38\pi \ \ (2.29\pi \text{ by the mid-ordinate rule with 4 strips})$

$V_2 = \pi \int_1^e \ln y \, dy = \pi \left[y \ln y - y \right]_1^e \ \ \text{(see question 6)}$

$= \pi$

(b) $V_1 = \pi \int_0^{\pi/2} \sin x \, dx = \pi$

$V_2 = \pi \int_0^1 (\sin^{-1} y^2)^2 \, dy \approx 0.27\pi$

(c) $V_1 = \pi \int_0^{\pi/3} \sec^2 x \, dx = \pi \left[\tan x \right]_0^{\pi/3} = \pi \sqrt{3}$

$V_2 = \pi \int_1^2 \left(\cos^{-1} \frac{1}{y} \right)^2 \, dy \approx 0.66\pi$

(d) $V_1 = \pi \int_0^{\pi/4} \tan^2 x \, dx = \pi \int_0^{\pi/4} (\sec^2 x - 1) \, dx$

$= \pi \left[\tan x - x \right]_0^{\pi/4} = \pi \left(1 - \frac{\pi}{4} \right)$

$V_2 = \pi \int_0^1 (\tan^{-1} x)^2 \, dx \approx 0.25\pi$

Polynomial approximations

1 The polynomial graphs fit that of ln $(1 + x)$ increasingly well.

2 (a) $1 - \dfrac{x}{2} + \dfrac{x^2}{24}$

$\cos \sqrt{0.2} \approx 0.90167$
$\cos \sqrt{0.4} \approx 0.8067$

(b) $\left[x - \dfrac{x^2}{4} + \dfrac{x^3}{72} \right]_0^{0.4} = 0.36089$. This is accurate to at least 4 s.f. since the fit is very good over most of the interval.

3 (a) $x^2 - \dfrac{x^4}{3} + \dfrac{2x^6}{45}$, neglecting higher powers

(b) $1 - 2x^2 + \dfrac{2x^4}{3} - \dfrac{4x^6}{45}$

(c) $\cos 2x = 1 - 2 \sin^2 x$

4 (a) $x^2 - \dfrac{x^4}{2} + \dfrac{x^6}{3} - \dfrac{x^8}{4}$; $1 - x^2 + x^4 - x^6 + x^8$

(b) $2x - 2x^3 + 2x^5 - 2x^7 = 2x (1 - x^2 + x^4 - x^6)$

$\dfrac{d}{dx} \left(\ln (1 + x^2) \right) = \dfrac{2x}{1 + x^2}$, from the chain rule

(c) $\left[\dfrac{x^3}{3} - \dfrac{x^5}{10} + \dfrac{x^7}{21} - \dfrac{x^9}{36} \right]_0^{0.5} = 0.03886$

$\left[x - \dfrac{x^3}{3} + \dfrac{x^5}{5} - \dfrac{x^7}{7} + \dfrac{x^9}{9} \right]_0^{0.5} = 0.46368$

(d) $\displaystyle\int_0^{0.5} (1 + x^2)^{-1} \, dx = \tan^{-1} 0.5 = 0.46365$

5 (a) $\displaystyle\int_0^{0.6} x \left(1 - \dfrac{x^2}{2} + \dfrac{x^4}{24} \right) dx = 0.16412$

$\displaystyle\int_0^{0.6} x \cos x \, dx = \left[x \sin x + \cos x \right]_0^{0.6} = 0.16412$, using integration by parts

(b) $\displaystyle\int_{0.2}^{0.8} \left(1 - \dfrac{x^2}{6} + \dfrac{x^4}{120} \right) dx = 0.57255$

$\dfrac{\sin x}{x}$ cannot be integrated exactly.

(c) $\displaystyle\int_0^{0.4}\left(1+x+\frac{x^2}{2}\right)\left(x-\frac{x^3}{6}\right)\,dx \approx \int_0^{0.4}\left(x+x^2+\frac{x^3}{3}\right)\,dx = 0.10347$

$\displaystyle\int_0^{0.4} e^x \sin x\,dx = \left[\frac{1}{2}(e^x \sin x - e^x \cos x)\right]_0^{0.4} = 0.10344$

(d) $\displaystyle\int_0^{0.7}\left(1+\frac{x^4}{2}-\frac{x^8}{8}\right)\,dx = 0.71625$

Direct integration is impossible.

(e) $\displaystyle\int_{-0.4}^{0.4}\left(x-\frac{x^2}{2}+\frac{x^3}{3}\right)\,dx = -0.02133$

$\displaystyle I = \int_{\ln 0.6}^{\ln 1.4} u\,e^u\,du$ since $x = e^u - 1$ and we replace dx by $e^u\,du$

$\displaystyle = \left[u\,e^u - e^u\right]_{\ln 0.6}^{\ln 1.4}$ using integration by parts

$= -0.02244$

The first 'missing' term of the polynomial approximation would contribute about –0.001 to the integral, hence the disparity between the answers.

6   (a) $1 - \dfrac{x^2}{2} = 3x \Rightarrow x^2 + 6x - 2 = 0$

$\Rightarrow x \approx 0.3166 \text{ or } -6.3166$

Graphs show that the negative answer is irrelevant; the Newton-Raphson method gives 0.31675 for the root.

(b)   Again there is only one root, a small positive number.

$1 + x + \dfrac{x^2}{2} = 2 - x$ gives $x \approx 0.4495$

The Newton-Raphson method gives 0.4429.

7   (a) $1 - \dfrac{x^2}{2} + \dfrac{x^4}{8} - \dfrac{x^6}{48}$

(b)   A calculator suggests a good fit from -1 to 1.

(c)   The program gives answers correct to at least 3 s.f. until x exceeds 1.1.

8   (a) $1 + \dfrac{1}{2}x^2 + \dfrac{\frac{1}{2}\times\frac{3}{2}}{2!}x^4 + \dfrac{\frac{1}{2}\times\frac{3}{2}\times\frac{5}{2}}{3!}x^6$

$x + \dfrac{1}{2}x^3 \div 3 + \dfrac{\frac{1}{2}\times\frac{3}{2}}{2!}x^5 \div 5 + \dfrac{\frac{1}{2}\times\frac{3}{2}\times\frac{5}{2}}{3!}x^7 \div 7$

$\sin^{-1} 0.3 \approx 0.30469$

(b) $t_1 = \frac{1}{2}x^3$, $t_2 = \frac{\frac{1}{2} \times \frac{3}{2}}{2!} x^5$, $t_3 = \frac{\frac{1}{2} \times \frac{3}{2} \times \frac{5}{2}}{3!} x^7$

(c)   Five terms are needed to achieve 8 s.f. accuracy.

(d)   0.52359878. $6 \times \sin^{-1} 0.5 = \pi$

9 $1 - x^2 + x^4 - x^6 + \ldots$

$x - \frac{x^3}{3} + \frac{x^5}{5} - \frac{x^7}{7} \ldots$

CASIO

```
? → X
X → T: X → S: X² → U
3 → D
Lbl 1
T × (− U) → T
S + T ÷ D → S ◢
D + 2 → D
Goto 1
```

TEXAS

```
Input X
X → T
X → S
X² → U
3 → D
Lbl 1
T × (− U) → T
S + T ÷ D → S
Disp S
D + 2 → D
Goto 1
```